MW00479870

# 20,000 OMS

## AND

# A CUP OF CHAI

SARVESH NAAGARI

20,000 Oms and a Cup of Chai by Sarvesh Naagari

Copyright © 2016 Gary R. Beebe Jr.

ISBN 9781682735688

All rights reserved. This book is protected under the copyright laws of the United States of America. This book may not be copied or reprinted for commercial gain or profit.

All direct references to the teachings of Alcoholics Anonymous taken from the Big Book of Alcoholics Anonymous, which is in the Public Domain.

Cover Design by Nancy Albert of New Brunswick, Canada

Do you have an inspiring story? Check out our web site and email your story to Sarvesh. We will post it and a photo to our blog for the community to read. Through sharing our growth and inspiration, we create a beautiful ripple effect in the world. If you enjoyed this story, please let people know about it and carry the message of hope and inspiration that it offers. Share it on Facebook, Instagram or write a review!

## Websites and Social Media

www.20000oms.com

www.sarveshnaagari.com

www.rippleyoga.com

## Facebook

www.facebook.com/rippleyoga

www.facebook.com/20000oms

www.facebook.com/sarveshnaagari

## Instagram

@rippleyoga

# Preface

I want to personally thank you for taking the time to read this story, which is my story, but to be succinct the story or my spirit and the journey that it has taken for the past 15 years. After reading it several times I have developed a sense of detachment from it and almost question whether all of this really happened. I assure you that it did. I went to great lengths in writing this to ensure that everything presented is factual and true to the best of my ability.

My hope is that this story helps people, plain and simple. I am not trying to win literary awards or to impress anyone with my vocabulary or writing skills. The goal was and is to carry the message of hope that my story depicts to the reader so that they can take the lessons and apply them to their own life or to the life of someone that is dear to them.

I also hope that the book can provide some insight into the mind of people that suffer from addiction, and not just to alcohol, as the psychology of addiction and recovery is patently similar independent of the addiction. Addiction has the same essence and very similar characteristics and results, even if the path is different. All addicts think they are terminally unique and it is not until they are in the recovery process that they realize that they are not.

This story is not about Yoga nor is it about alcoholism or the recovery from addiction. They are the spiritual tools that I used and use daily in my life to both overcome life's problems and to grow spiritually. They are a way of life and the similarities between the two disciplines are eerily similar in theory and practice, even though the taxonomy used to describe them is completely different.

When reading this story I hope that the reader can look past the characteristics described and see the essence of the recovery and growth of the spirit. Alcoholism can be replaced with any of a myriad of personal challenges that we all have and need to overcome as human beings, and we must realize that our internal spirit and our virtue is our true strength. And while the problem can be easily substituted in this story, so can the solution to any true spiritual program. Please keep an open mind and I hope that you enjoy the true and inspirational story of my spirit. You are welcome and encouraged to carry the message of this story to anyone you think could benefit in their life.

There are certain terms used in this story that may be new to the reader, and while I have been careful to define them in the text of the story, oftentimes additional reference is necessary. All of these terms are in *italic and bold* and can be referenced in the glossary in the back of the book.

I would also like to note that my name was Gary, and at the end of the Yoga training in India I was given the name Sarvesh Naagari by my Guru. The name has multiple and deep meanings and was chosen for me based on my spiritual potential. It is in the spirit of this name and the beauty of this gift of my name that I present this story to you.

In Unity and Love,

Sarvesh

# What is Yoga?

This can be a challenging question in today's world, in particular in Western culture where Yoga very often does not resemble Yoga at all, but a physical fitness class that is called Yoga. As a culture, we have a tendency to rename or redefine things to fit our intents and purposes, particularly when there is money involved. With that being said, your perception of Yoga is left entirely up to you.

For the purpose of this story, I would like to provide some context on what Yoga is as defined in this book and as I teach it. This will help the reader to better understand the concepts presented in this story.

Yoga is a way of life. It is not something that is done once or twice a week at a studio and then left by the wayside. Yoga is a practice that becomes a discipline that we eventually transcend to a point of love. Once we make this transcendence, we become Yoga and we no longer do it or practice it. What this implies is that Yoga is more than just Asana, or the physical practice, and this is inherently true. When we are living Yoga, we are in a state of awareness of our behaviors, awareness of our physical interactions with the world around us and our state of being. We are aware of our energy and in control of our sensory inputs. In short, we have conscious awareness of our existence rather than reactionary impulse. This awakening is gained through practice of all the limbs of Yoga and is also a path to virtue and happiness.

I hope that this simple definition helps the reader in the clarification and context of this story.

# Gratitude

I would like to thank Norman Schwagler for taking the time and making the strenuous effort to edit this work. Norman is both a dear friend and a cousin. We are the nomads of the family, leaving Buffalo, NY to travel here and there, seeing the world and sharing our experiences as we go. In addition to being an English teacher for over 20 years, he is a fabulous musician and a wonderful human being.

The India portion of this story takes place at the ICYER at Ananda Ashram in Pondicherry, India during their famous six-month teacher training program. It is a limited and challenging program and not for the faint of spirit, but the rewards are more than any one human can ask. The loving attention that is given to the teachings and the environment by Yogacharini Meenakshi Devi Bhavanani, Director and Resident Acharya, ICYER at Ananda Ashram and Yogacharya Dr Ananda Balayogi Bhavanani, Chairman, ICYER at Ananda Ashram is truly unique and special. I have utmost and profound respect for them, the teachings of Yogamaharishi Dr Swami Gitananda Giri Guru Maharaj, Founder, ICYER at Ananda Ashram and the Rishiculture Yoga lineage in this Paramparya and my heart is filled with gratitude for the experience.

I would also like to thank the classmates that were with me in the teacher training program. There were 7 of us total and since there were so few of us, I have chosen not to put their names in this section. But you all know who you are and I am grateful to each of you for what you taught me and for holding the mirror up to me while we lived together at the ashram.

Thank you to Nancy Albert for designing the cover of the book and keeping it simple, the team at Integra in Pondicherry for the layout and e-file creation.

Many thanks go to all the people who took the time to read the book before it was published and provided honest feedback. Your feedback was incredible and helped keep me on the straight and narrow.

I cannot thank enough my family for supporting me both in leaving the country for 6 months and in this project.

It is impossible to write a story about the life that one has experienced without thanking everyone that has touched that life. So thank you to everyone I have met in my lifetime. Everyone that crosses our path does so for a reason, to help us learn some lesson of the universe, and I am grateful for all my teachers.

I would also like to thank all the instructors at Ripple Yoga while I was away for continuing to carry the message of Yoga to the community in my absence.

And finally I offer my gratitude, thanks and love to Kim who ran the Yoga studio in Seattle while I was gone. It was a lot to ask and she more than rose to the occasion and put her loving touch and energy into the Yoga community at Ripple Yoga. I love you angel.

In Unity and Love,

S.N.

*For Gary and Taree*
*My Inspiration*

# Part One

## *Hell Is Not Where We Go When We Die... ...*

## Chapter 1 - Seven Years Ago

The cat kept walking in circles around the lip of the tub, ignoring the body that was slumped into it. The body looked to be in its fifties with matted grey brown hair and eyes that were bloodshot and partially rolled into the back of its head. The ribs were protruding from the sides of the body and if the cat had a xylophone hammer it could have chimed the ribs in a clear tone. The face was unshaven with patches of grey hair that strained to grow through the malnourished state of the body and the tongue was partially lolled out to the side, coated with a sickly dry, white film. The chest was not visibly moving with breath although a light wisp of fog escaped from the mouth every once in a while suggesting a shallow, erratic breathing pattern.

The body was mine, and it was beaten to within an inch of its life. What from, I could not remember as I was unable to move anything except my eyes. While I wasn't paralyzed completely, the effort of moving was so intense and so difficult and the body so heavy that I couldn't bring my mind to make it happen. The room I was in was unfamiliar. It appeared I had been dropped into a large claw foot tub which was an expensive white porcelain model with a hard water stain at the outer limit of my vision. I could sense that there was tepid water rising up to about the lower area of my back and I was completely naked. The room felt cold and I could see my staggered breath escaping from my mouth.

There were no attachments to the tub that could be seen and the room stretched into nothingness in the three directions that I could see. Within this nothingness I could see a light mist falling that I could not feel. There was no ceiling as it stretched up into the same nothingness as the room. The bright white cat kept circling the rim of the off-white tub and each time it passed my leg that was draped over the outside of the tub it would walk over it as if it were a natural part of the landscape. The cat had mud yellow eyes with no pupils but never turned its head in any direction other than where it was going. Circling, circling, and circling. Its hair bristled up and down with each breath and it also was unaffected by the mist falling in the room.

I kept having a recurring thought that I was dead and that this seemed like an odd reception room to the eternal. It seemed even in death I couldn't contain my twisted sense of humor. With all the mental and physical strength I could muster I tried to lift and turn my head to get a glance of what was behind me. This effort failed and the exhaustion of doing so caused me to black out.

Some indeterminable time later I came to and nothing had changed including the position of my body. It was exactly, and it seemed to the millimeter, where it had been before. There was no sense of time so before could have been thirty seconds or thirty hours for all I knew. The thoughts coming to me were just as slow as the cold of the room.

I finally gave up on attempting movement and was able to create a barely audible whisper.

"Am I dead?"

Nothing happened. The only sound in the room was the light mist which reminded me of a light rain on a summer day at a lake, where there is a beautiful perception of the rainfall connecting and uniting with the larger body of the lake, a uniting of common elements that is more of a feeling than a sound. I asked again and was able to ask a little more audibly.

"Am I dead?"

"Almost," a soft voice said. At least I think that's what it said. It was a reassuring voice; that of a most trusted adult to a child. That one adult in every child's life outside of the parents that is trusted more than any other. Maybe it is a teacher, maybe it is a grandparent, maybe it is a neighbor, but when hearing the voice of that person it immediately brings the entire being to a place of ease and trust.

"Almost," I could only repeat the answer.

"Yes. You will die very soon." The voice was still soft but now had a sense of urgency to it, which was matched by my sense of urgency to not be here any longer, wherever here was. The voice also had a very familiar, colloquial quality. The voice reminded me of the most loving of fathers speaking to his only child who had just performed a balancing act on the side of a very deep well and had nearly toppled into the nothingness; the father trying to reassure the child that he was now safe but at the same time that the boy should pay attention to his surroundings. The care in the voice was deep and meaningful, carrying a weight that bore deep into the core of the heart.

"Where is this?" The presentation of each thought was a titanic struggle, each time sucking the energy and will from my being.

"A small rarely used part of your mind with a random collection of fears playing on the same loop. It is like a dream sequence. There is no such thing as time here, at least as you consciously understand it. And it isn't really a place at all, so far as you understand the concept of space."

"So I am dreaming." I closed my eyes and started to pray to a God that I didn't believe in to make this stop.

"You are not dreaming. You are hallucinating."

3

"Hallucinating?" It was an immense struggle just to get one or two words to escape my lips.

"You don't remember anything right now. Your only reality is here, and this is the only one that matters anyway. And it only matters because I am here with you. And that is only going to matter for a very short period of time." The voice was very soothing, but it was disturbing that it kept saying *close to death*. I had a vague recollection that this was exactly what I wanted.

"Who are you?" I considered myself to be a rather intelligent human being and in this place, which I refused to accept as a place in my mind, I could only muster 3 to 4 word questions much like a 3-year-old who is just learning to speak coherently.

"I am you." The voice replied calmly. The calmer the voice was, the more disconnected I seemed to feel. "I am your deepest you, your divine self."

"OK" I felt empty. There was no argument, no resolve, just a bankruptcy of all things human. As consciousness was beginning to slip away I could hear an ambulance siren in the distance growing nearer.

"The universe has decided that you should be spared, that the body you (we) chose to inhabit has a purpose. We cannot leave this body until that purpose is fulfilled."

# Chapter 2

"I'm sorry, while I think that is a beautiful offer and you have a wonderful business idea, I am just not interested at this time. In fact, I am getting ready for a flight. I am leaving for India for 6 months to study Yoga at an ashram. Have a wonderful day." I hung up the phone and looked over to Kim. She was trying her best to hold it together but I knew the tears would come. For me too, leaving for India for 6 months was a big deal, especially given that we had just met 4 months prior.

"Who was that baby?" She had her hair up in a ponytail high up on her head. It swished from ear to ear when she talked and this look always made me smile.

"I was just offered $5 M dollars over the next 5 years to be the President and CEO of a consulting company. I turned it down." I said this with the nonchalance of someone ordering their daily coffee.

She chuckled and with no surprise in her voice, "I bet the guy was quite shocked."

I grabbed the keys and began to roll my luggage out the door, guitar case in one hand, taking one last glance at our apartment in Seattle before heading off to India. "Indeed he was, my love. Indeed, he was."

As we drove to the airport I thought of the enormity of what had happened in the past few months to both our lives. We had just met at a Yoga festival 4 months prior, and had become inseparable. We met 2,500 miles away from Seattle near her home in Boston and the meeting was filled with so many coincidences that we were convinced it was universal intervention. We clicked so immediately and so deeply that she decided to move out West and manage my business during this 6 month adventure to India. I was torn in so many directions as my eyes tried to stay focused on the road. Was I making the correct decision to leave this beautiful woman, whom I loved so deeply, so soon after not only just meeting but her living in an entirely new city uprooted from her family and friends? Was I making the right decision to have her running the business in my absence? My heart already hurt with the thought of being apart and these thoughts further complicated the emotional responses. It was going to be a turbulent flight independent of the airplane ride.

Standing on the curb of the departure drop off at Seattle-Tacoma International Airport looking at her stunning beauty, it finally hit me that I wouldn't see her again for 6 months. She was smiling and crying at the same time, making a heart shape with her hands, her thumbs touching on the bottom between her breasts and the top fingers curled together. Tears welled up within me as I blew her a kiss and tried to be strong as I turned to enter the airport.

The flight to India was 18 hours with one connection followed by a three hour drive to my final destination. I would be living at a Yoga Ashram for 6 months studying under the guidance of a guru in what is called a Gurukula. This translates as the house of the guru where the students share the quarters with the guru and his family, and become part of the family.

I had no idea what to expect and really wasn't sure why I was going. There had been a lot of this in my life over the past 7 years. I was simply given direction from the universe and followed it, without question. This direction came in the form of very strong thoughts in my head and heart and I learned at some point that this voice was my teacher within. Some people call it "God" talking to them, some call it intuition, but whatever the name, it was something that I had learned to trust and follow.  In fact, it has been said that I follow this to a fault.

As I settled into the seat on the plane I pondered the journey that lay before me.  I had made a conscious decision to leave behind a yoga studio that I had built with my own two hands and nurtured to life for the past 2 years, a new-found girlfriend that had left her life and moved 2,500 miles to be with me just 2 short months ago just so that I could up and leave her for six months.  I left my consulting practice, which was actually a joyous occasion, and all the hobbies and friends in Seattle.  I left my family, who despite living on the East coast, I had managed to see extensively during the past year.

And despite some calling for a lunacy commission to be commenced on my behalf, it felt like exactly the right thing to do.  The rubber room would have to wait, at least for six months!  I thought of the love that I had for this woman who just entered my life, and the concept that we were twin flames, separated souls reunited for a purpose, and how that felt right in the heart as well.  We've known each other for either four months or 1,000 years, we couldn't decide.

The waters of the universe move fast, and I had decided to jump headfirst into the middle of the current and flow with it some seven years ago.  Before that, I spent twenty plus years swimming against the current, and my life ended up a living hell.  I wanted to use this time at the ashram to review my life up to this point, to see if I could create some distance and objectivity and analyze what had happened; to see if some sense could be made of the cause and effect.

Self-study is good for the soul, and I intended to use the time and space, physically and mentally, that the ashram provided to do just that.  And as I was considering cause and effect, it reminded me that it is said that you can break the laws of man, but you can only bend cosmic law.  And while bending cosmic law can hurt you and those around you, breaking cosmic law will kill you.

This cosmic law, or Karma as it is also known, is the law of cause and effect.  We live so blindly and so unaware of how the universe works that we don't realize that for every action that we take, there is an equal and opposite reaction.  This is not just the law of Karma; it is a principle of physics.  The issue with Karma is that we can't always see the cause and begin to blame the effects of our lives on others, rather than accepting responsibility for the effects in our lives.  As the plane lifted its wheels and we headed on our way, I dozed off pondering how I pushed cosmic law, or Karma, to its breaking point, and how that had almost killed me.

Beach music was pumping through the amplifiers and the DJ was in good form.  It was 7:00 am on Sunday morning and the pace was picking up at the resort bar in this small town in Delaware famous for its Sunday morning fracas.  Sunday, bloody Sunday was in full swing and the throng of shirtless and tanned men, some who took great pride in their abs and some who took great pride in their beer guts, reveled with bikini clad women trying to catch the attention of anyone cool enough to chat with them.  To the left of the entrance tables were jammed with hung-over patrons ordering the signature dish: eggs benedict with blue crab meat and their first drink of the day to take the edge off the previous evening's party.

To the right stretched a long wall with over 500 ingredients to make a Bloody Mary, a favorite vodka based drink of the hung-over.  Order a Bloody Mary, receive a glass of vodka, and then go make it yourself!  The bar was filled with people smoking and partying as if Saturday night never ended, and for some of them it didn't.

This beach was an adult playground, the type of place where people went to escape their office jobs; escape the city life.  Alcohol was a way of life here, and the average house held 25 people each weekend throughout the summer.  Happy hour started at 4:00 each day and rolled into the evening; the bars closed at 1:00 am and then the parties transitioned to the various houses packed into the thin 4 block stretch from beach to bay.  From Memorial Day to Labor Day, from Friday to Sunday, this was the agenda, and it was more than just a destination, it was a way of life.

By 7:30 am on this particular Sunday I was on my third beer. Life was amazing. I smiled across the room at my fiancée through the throng of revelers. She was heavily emoting about something, her arms flailing wildly as her smiling blue eyes captured the attention of every guy within sight. Her dark hair was in a tail and it whooshed across her bare back down by the bikini strap. We had met at this beach some years earlier and had gotten engaged at this beach on New Year's Eve. This place had become a part of our DNA.

Karly and I were building quite a life together. She had started her own graphic design business and I was working as a VP of Finance for a startup company outside of Washington, DC. We had recently purchased a townhouse with a cool and contemporary floor plan in the suburbs located on a lush and quaint golf course. We hosted people for dinners and social events all year round and for 2 people in their late 20's, life was grand. We worked hard during the week and played harder on weekends and neither noticed nor thought about the amount we drank or smoked.

We had shared a beautiful routine together for the past 2 years since she had moved from New York City to join me in D.C. On weeknights, we would cook at home 2 nights and eat out at a local restaurant one night. When at home, we would usually share a bottle of wine and when it was nice out, eat out on the deck listening to the stereo through the outdoor speakers. We either cooked together or for each other, each of us enjoying the duty. We had become foodies of sorts, as a couple years' prior I was a partner in a fine dining restaurant in one of the wealthier suburbs of Northern Virginia.

The restaurant had eventually run its course and closed, but for four years it was nice to say that I was a partner in it and eat there for free. Not a bad badge of honor for a twenty-something up and coming business guru. Karly and I had taken to high-end dining and had taken full advantage of the restaurant when we met even extending it to other fine dining establishments in the D.C. area. We would book reservations at different places on a Friday night and mention that we were partners in the establishment in Virginia and usually get special treatment such as sitting at the chef's table, complimentary wine, appetizers or desserts.

Through this love of food, we began to try to replicate restaurant menus at home, attempting to guess the ingredients and recreate the dishes. Wine or beer pairing with the dish was imperative, and this hobby was something that was bringing us closer together. We had become the perfect socialite couple, in our minds the couple that everyone wanted to be, and to be with.

"You're late!" I was startled out of this daydream by the DJ. I had heard him say this 100 times in between songs in the general direction of whoever had just walked in the door. It always got a laugh. The beach party would last until noon or about 7-8 beers and we would meander back to the beach house or down to the ocean for a nap before heading back to the city. It was a beautiful lifestyle and one that I wished could continue forever. However, forever was coming faster than I anticipated.

I always called life for Karly and me the roaring twenties. Life was a grand chorus of work hard and play harder, chasing the American dream of a hot wife, a house on a golf course and a fast car. Children would follow, and I would eventually secure my birthright of leading a company to great success, my calm leadership and skill in business being a match for no one. I would be able to retire at an early age (forty, I hoped) and live a life of pampered luxury raising my kids and being the perfect father. That was the plan, I had thought. The universe, on the other hand, had other plans for me.

# Chapter 4

It felt odd getting off the plane and realizing that it was 2 days later. In real time, 20 ½ hours had passed but it was early Tuesday morning and I had left on Sunday afternoon. As with all international arrivals, it took forever to get through customs but I felt pretty good after such a long stretch flight. I had travelled considerably internationally and have never been able to tell that I am in a different country from the airport. It is like the blueprint for airport design is just duplicated from country to country and city to city right down to the glum civil servant that checks your passport. I was 5th in line, and it took a solid 10 minutes to process each person with at least 4 minutes apportioned to glaring with serious eyes over very serious looking glasses at the weary traveler's passport.

It is always after going through customs and exiting the controlled area of the airport that the realization hits that it is a foreign country. In India, it was apparent immediately because of the blast of heat, my white skin radiating against everyone else's brown skin, and the excessive number of taxi drivers who did not have taxis. Fortunately, the ashram had arranged a driver for me, who was diligently holding up a sign with my name on it. It was 3:00 in the morning and he didn't look very happy to be picking up a total stranger at the airport 3 hours away from his warm bed.

It was a 3 plus hour drive from the airport despite it being only 160 kilometers. This is because there are minor issues with the roads in India, starting with there are few roads and the ones that connect major metropolis to major metropolis only have 2 lanes. And cows. And dogs, goats, bicycles, scooters, ox drawn carriages, buses, trucks and a few cars; and this is at 3:30 in the morning! And not even a shred of traffic law, at least that anyone follows. It was also pouring rain. They also drive on the opposite side of the road, so to me the drive was completely unnerving. We almost hit 3 cows. I have no idea how the driver could see with the rain, the oncoming traffic and the milieu of insanity on the roadway.

We arrived at the ashram at 7:30 am and I was greeted by a friendly woman who I would later learn was one of our teachers. She had an Eastern European accent and was tall with light brown hair in a long ponytail. Her features showed a lot of inner strength and I could feel a very kind energy to her. She also seemed very tired. Her eyes though were a steel blue and quite alive. After exchanging introductions, I was shown to a room that would be my home for the next six months and shown the location of the shower, and asked to be ready for breakfast in 90 minutes so that I could meet some of the other students.

The ashram is beautiful and spacious reflecting the tropical climate and its natural environment, located on the Bay of Bengal on the Southeast coast of India. A mere 20 years ago the beach was 500 meters from the ashram to the shoreline. Tsunamis, global warming and cyclones have moved the ocean to within 10 meters of the back gate of the ashram. In fact, the concrete wall that housed the back gate of the ashram was knocked down by a tsunami a few years ago and is now a fence. A retaining wall has been built most of the length of the beach as the ocean presses ever further in. I imagine that one day in the near future this small fishing town and the ashram will no longer be as the ocean will reclaim this part of India.

The entry to the ashram opens to 30 foot ceilings in the main practice room, which I was informed by the teacher that we don't practice in except for when there is heavy rain. It is tiled with dark green ceramic tiles which measure one square meter each. The tiles are always cool to the touch and the energy moves up through the feet whenever we care to notice such things. The room is decorated with the many Hindu Gods and Goddesses, as well as many pictures and tributes to the Guru and his late Guru. The hall moves into a foyer which is used for evening *Satsangha*, which is time that the students spend in the evening learning from the Guru and listening to stories and teachings. The other exit from the main hall leads into an outdoor atrium where the senior teachers are housed. The entire ashram is open air and intentionally opens to nature. It is designed in every aspect to be in harmony with its natural surroundings.

From the *Satsangha* foyer, there are stairs up to the family living quarters. This ashram is a true Gurukula, which means a house of the guru and the students become part of the family for the time that they cohabitate. The Gurukula experience is both unique and rare in today's world. In the old days, this was how the knowledge of Yoga was transferred from Guru to student (or Chela or seeker), by word of mouth with the student living in close quarters with the Guru.

Past the stairs to the living quarters are the student and guest dining hall, another outdoor atrium where the female students are housed, and the door to the backyard. Another set of stairs leads upstairs to a practice room for when it rains, a hut with coconut leaves as a roof for practice of Pranayama, and the rooms where the male students are housed. There is also a library upstairs and another outdoor deck facing the ocean (east) where we practice morning Hatha Yoga at sunrise.

Out the back door is a spacious yard with statues and fruit trees, clothes lines and an eight sided hut dedicated to Patanjali, who codified the practice of Yoga in the Yoga Sutras. There are 8 limbs, or steps, in the practice of Yoga under the Patanjali theorem. These 8 limbs are a design for living a spiritual life and growing oneself in spirit, and are Yama (restraint), Niyama (morals), Asana (State of being), Pranayama (Energy Control), Pratyahara (Control of Senses), Dharana (Concentration), Dyana (Meditation) and Samadhi (Cosmic Consciousness).

Inside the Patanjali hut, we practice chanting and have lectures from the Guru, which is open air. The ashram is striking because it so in tune with nature and the natural surroundings. Even with the ocean moving closer, the sound of the waves coming to shore at night is a seamless lullaby. Birds of many species are heard although these days there are mostly crows, which I equate in volume and number to gulls on just about any beach on the east coast of America. There are 4 dogs at the ashram, lizards, mice, and monkeys, insects of every hue on the spectrum, frogs and just outside the walls cows, chickens and goats. Everything is in harmony and the circle of life amongst all the living beings is both understood and deeply appreciated. I feel truly blessed to be here.

I could also sense immediately that this was not going to be Yoga as I was accustomed to in the West. Yoga in the West has largely become a callisthenic exercise performing shapes with the body to a music playlist. Yoga is so much more than that and while there are a lot of definitions of Yoga, this ashram believes that Yoga is a way of life and a form of conscious evolution. The shapes are used as a means to this end. I would learn in the next six months that it was far more than I could possibly imagine, forever changing the way I think about Yoga and forever changing the way I live my life.

Karly's piercing blue eyes flared as she pointed the spatula at me. Her lips were thin anyway but when she was angry they became almost unnoticeable as they were pulled back under her teeth. Her face was red and she was almost in tears from the anger.

"Don't EVER tell me how to cook fish. I will do this however I want and if you don't like it, go screw yourself." The spatula was dripping some type of sauce on the floor. I supposed that this would be my fault as well. Everything was my fault, according to her.

"The counselor said that you need to stop trying to control my behavior." This had been my usual smart-ass remark, which was to use the counselor's sage advice against her. We had started to see a relationship counselor and our sessions, in my opinion, were a complete waste of time and money. Karly always left crying and I was always angry. No solutions were reached.

"Gary, you are the most stubborn and unreasonable human being ever. You don't listen, and all you do is sit around and drink. Why don't you get a job?" She loved to point out how lazy I was, or how lazy she thought I was.

The reality was that I lost my job just after we got back from Costa Rica. I was unsure why; the CEO of the company just showed up at the house and terminated me with one month of severance. He said that he needed to hire someone who could be in New Hampshire full time rather than shuttling me back and forth from Washington, DC twice a month. I suspected that wasn't the real reason but it didn't matter. I would land on my feet, someone with my talent always did.  That was 4 weeks ago and I was unable to find work up to that point.  We were running out of money too.  I mostly spent my time sitting around drinking after spending a couple hours in the morning looking for work.  I deserved that though.  I had worked my ass off the past 3 years to give us the lifestyle we had.  And what had she done?

"At least I work and contribute around here.  I have no idea what the hell you have been doing the past 3 years."  This was cruel to say but there was truth to it.  She had started a graphic design business but earned almost no income from it.  In all honesty, that didn't bother me, because all I wanted was her happiness, but in the heat of the moment I was being cruel, and knew it.

"Why don't you just go sit outside and smoke and drink?"  She was crying now, too upset to be angry, too frustrated for any other emotion so the tears started to flow.  She was broken, and I had broken her.  I won the argument, and I was keeping score.

Good.  She treats me like shit, and doesn't love me anyway.  Not sure why I continue to bother.  I went outside, opened a beer and had a cigarette.

It was warm and muggy out, a typical summer evening in Northern Virginia.  Even after seven or eight beers these arguments always made my mind clear.  I wondered where her happiness had gone.  For the past 6-9 months she had become progressively unhappier with everything, nagging and complaining incessantly.  I couldn't work hard enough, earn enough or take enough vacations.  We had just gotten back from Costa Rica about a month ago and she was miserable on the entire trip.  I assured myself that I hadn't changed a bit since we met.  What you see is what you get with me.  I wasn't sure what was bringing on the change in her.  Just as this was crossing my mind she came out with a glass of wine, sat down and lit a cigarette.  Ignoring that I was even sitting in the same hemisphere, she sat there with her eyes insanely focused on the side of the house. I could feel her anger looking for an exit. If I dared say one thing, nothing short of Armageddon was coming my way, which would eventually be followed by tears and her then isolating herself in the bedroom. There was so much drama in our lives these days. I really wish she could get her head screwed back on straight.

"I'm moving out." When she finally looked at me this is what she said. She said it flatly, and very matter of fact. This decision had been made, it seemed. I was sure she already knew where she was going. For one of the few times in my life, I had no words.

"It's not about the damn fish," she continued. And rather than being emotional and irrational, she was crystal clear. The higher parts of her brain were in control, for this part of the conversation at least. "You are insufferable. You are not the same person that I fell in love with. You don't want to do anything other than go to that shithole bar every night and get wasted. You lost your job, and don't seem to be putting much of an effort into getting a new one. You barely even look at me. We don't have sex. You are completely emotionally unavailable. I cannot accept you the way you are any longer and I am moving out. Honestly, I have no idea what is actually wrong with you, but I suggest that you figure it out, because you have turned into an egotistical, self-righteous ass. You are also incredibly selfish, which is odd because when we met you were one of the most kind and giving people I ever met. It was one of the traits I loved about you. But over the past year or so, you have gotten more and more selfish each day. You barely give me the time of day and we live together. You hurt me with your emotional unavailability every day, and I am not going to take it anymore. I try to talk to you and you just blame me and try to turn everything on me. Look in the damn mirror once in a while." She was past anger and into logical reasoning and the list she read off fell on me like a judge reading a sentence to a long time criminal. Denial and anger were fighting for the use of my vocal chords at the same time and pain and anguish were not far behind.

"You leave me you will actually have to get a job." That is all I could muster. All I could do was insult her, and dig the knife in where I knew it hurt the most. It was self-righteous and cruel, and I knew it.

"I would rather get a job or move back to New York and live with my parents than live with you another ten seconds. You are cruel and insensitive. You are just mean and filled with hate. And the worse thing is, you don't hate me, you hate you. And then you just project that hate on everyone around you. You are just awful. Get help with whatever is going on inside your head. You are insane." Now she was crying. Her hands were shaking terribly and she was fumbling to try to light another cigarette. Tears streamed down her thin face and high cheekbones. The eye liner was running off to the corners. She had a little button nose and it was stuffy and running at the same time as she tried to project what she wanted to say. I was deeply satisfied with the pain she was experiencing; she deserved it for her irrational judgment of me. I had been supporting her for four years, how dare she talk to me like this? I walked into the house to get another beer. When I came out it seemed she had regained some of her composure. She was staring at me now with open hatred as I coolly sat down and lit a cigarette. I could feel the logic swelling within me to win this argument, it was being pieced together like a complex puzzle made easy by my superior brain.

"You sit there and read off this list of things wrong with me. Who are you to judge me! The counselor said point blank that you needed to stop trying to control me. You make me go to eight counseling sessions, that I of course had to pay for, and then you refuse to take the guidance of the counselor. This is your entire fault, if you weren't so damn controlling we wouldn't be having this conversation. See, I am exactly the same as I was when we met; you just keep trying to control me and change me into something I am not.  Very typical if you ask me."  It was a beautiful rebuttal.  It had logic, made sense and brought in the objective third party.  Lord knows she wasn't going to listen to me.

"You are an ass."  She was back to unemotional Karly.  "The counselor said each and every thing that I just listed out to you but of course you take the *one thing* that she said for me to work on and blame the entire relationship on that.  You are a complete ass."

It seems I had lost the argument.  She moved out a week later.  I got drunk, and started to blame God and the universe for my problems, since she was no longer there to blame.  By some bizarre twist of fate, I also found out a week later that I would be interviewing for a job in Seattle, Washington.

# Chapter 6

In the yoga ashram, routine is a part of life. Consistency and devotion are required in the practice of yoga and we were going to get both in large doses during our stay. We were given a schedule sheet from the teacher on the first day identifying our routine. Teachers who had previously studied and completed the 6-month course would lead some classes and the Guru would lead others, depending on scheduling.

Our schedule was highly repetitive and structured and I remember thinking that it would be very challenging for a person of poor discipline or an unstructured life. I didn't have a lot of structure in my life but

*Daily Schedule*

*5:00 am - Wake Up Bell*

*5:30 am - Morning Arthi*

*5:35 am - Morning Meditation*

*6:00 am - Hatha Yoga*

*8:00 am - Breakfast*

*9:00 am - Karma Yoga*

*10:00 am - Free Time*

*11:00 am - Pranayama*

*1:00 pm - Lunch*

*2:00 pm - Free Time*

*4:30 pm - Mantra*

*6:00 pm - Dinner*

*7:00 pm - Bajans (Singing)*

did have discipline. Our typical schedule looked like this five days a week. We had one day off where we only practiced Hatha Yoga and in the evening had singing classes and on Sundays we practiced Yoga Therapy and chanting only. The schedule was demanding, unyielding and repetitive. It is through this discipline and regular practice that we gain self-awareness, or the practice of **Swadiyaya**, which is self-examination. We were taught that self-awareness is the greatest gift that we can offer the universe as a human being.

Morning and evening Arthi are Hindu rituals more than Yogic and they are dedications and brief chanting to the divine, showing gratitude for the Yoga lineage and offering peace to the universe. We are expected to observe Mauna (silence) for ten minutes before each practice and after the Mantra class each day. Mauna is observed as a time of reflection and a time to practice the discipline of not speaking. This discipline turns into becoming a better listener.

After morning Arthi, we sit outside facing the ocean east towards the sunrise. It is still dark. This is called the time of the divine or God's time, just before sunrise, and it is utilized for meditation and reflection. It is quiet out on the deck at this time, only the sound of the gentle waves of the ocean rolling in from the east, and an occasional rooster cock-a-doodle-dooing in the background signaling that dawn in approaching. As we sit, the energy of this place is evident in its synergy with nature. This energy not something that is so prevalent in western culture, and even with the booming population in India, this connection with Mother Earth can still be felt. As the rotation of the earth brings southeastern India closer to sunrise, the cacophony of life begins to awaken. Crows begin their endless cawing, roosters continue to cock-a-doodle-do, the flies wake up from their evening slumber and begin to buzz around us and the gentle sound of Ooooooommmmm from the teacher signals that it is time to begin our Hatha practice. We can just see the sun peeking over the horizon, the powerful red aura of the morning light beginning to show itself.

Hatha Yoga is the practice of physical postures, utilizing breath to embody the posture. The physical practice of Yoga is intended to develop a unity or oneness with the universe, by embodying the shapes that we make with our body. We practice Hatha to eventually move beyond our body. Yoga believes that we are reincarnated and have been reincarnated many thousands of times and we will continue to be reincarnated until we have learned all the lessons in life that we must learn. Another way of putting this is that we are continually reborn until we have burned all of our Karma. And then at that point, we are reunited with the divine. This is also the Hindu belief system. Yoga stemmed from Hinduism but it is not Hinduism; Yoga believes in no religion because it believes in oneness of everything, and by that definition, different religions cannot exist because they represent a duality of man.

Once we complete Hatha practice, which lasts for two hours, we have a breakfast that is South Indian, vegetarian and usually included a combination of chutney, dosa and idlee. The food is always prepared and served Sattvic, which means fresh and made with positive intent, and is prepared to be agreeable and gentle on the digestive system. We always have fresh fruit and chai with breakfast as well plus a lot of dahl, which is a good source of protein on our vegetarian diet.

Karma yoga follows breakfast, and is a list of duties that we provide to the ashram as upkeep of our living quarters. Performing service for others with the expectation of nothing in return is one of the paths to enlightenment, and we are expected to perform an hour of Karma Yoga work a day. These jobs vary and some of them require us to clean and do chores while others require us to support the teachers by setting up the practice rooms in advance of each practice. One person is chosen to ring all the bells before classes. Our Karma Yoga duties shift from person to person month to month.

We then have an hour of free time before we begin our Pranayama practice. This is a two-hour class where we practice breathing techniques. Pranayama means to control energy, and the primary source of energy is the breath. The benefits of proper breathing and Pranayama are endless and include a longer, happier, healthier life, cleansing of the nervous system, cleansing of the joints, lower heart rate and blood pressure and disease prevention. It is an amazing practice and one that is almost completely overlooked in the West, because of the obsession with the physical appearance and Asana practice. It is unfortunate but it very challenging to get a Westerner to practice Pranayama because they don't feel like they are practicing and it doesn't fit the definition of Yoga as they know it.

Once we have completed Pranayama we have lunch and then are free until 4:30 in the afternoon. At 4:30 we have Mantra class which is also a lecture from the Guru. We learn the Yoga Sutras and many different chants and mantras. It is a beautiful experience to hear a person of such amazing knowledge and wisdom share his teachings with us and the teachings of the gurus before him as each teaching penetrates our existence and the energy of the teaching stays with us for later contemplation and practice

We then have dinner which was always light and consisted of fresh fruit and soup and after dinner we spend about 30 minutes singing Bajans, which are Cartanaic Indian songs written about devotion. We then have evening *Satsangha*, which is a discussion with the Guru on the overall nature of our studies and additional direction on ashram life. From there, we have evening arthi and bedtime, with enough time to sleep and do it all again the following morning. Thank God for Thursdays, that is our day off!

The plane taxied down the runway of Washington, DC National Airport for its one way first class flight to Seattle. I smiled as I sipped a hand crafted IPA lager feeling confident in the new start to my life. Only 34 years old, hired into a leadership role in a large multi-national corporation! I could leave all the troubles of DC behind me; the failed relationship, the lack of jobs available to someone with my unique and varied skills, and the house with too many memories.

The real- estate market was booming in DC and I would sell the house at a fantastic gain which would be reinvested in a bigger house in Seattle. That, coupled with my handsome salary and stock options in the new role put me well on the path to retirement in my forties. Some smart investments and just being myself in the new role were all that stood between me and being a working stiff for the rest of my life.

A clear thought then entered my addled mind. A little more than half drunk for the flight, there were almost problems getting through security. I blamed it on the tightening of security due to the September 11th terrorist attacks and the fact that I had a one way first class ticket, but the reality was that I was probably considered too drunk to fly. I realized that I had almost blown the interview 30 days earlier because of a wicked hangover and probably only got the job because an ex-associate was the hiring manager. Clear thoughts like that didn't stay in my head often, so it was discharged in favor of how amazing I was, and how much I deserved the role. The role was offered a week after the interview and plans were made. The house was put on the market and off to the West Coast it was.

There was one minor issue that had to be dealt with upon arrival in Seattle. It was a bump in the road to success, to be certain, but one that would be dealt with assurance and confidence. A month prior to the interview, I had been pulled over for driving under the influence of alcohol at more than twice the legal limit. Virginia had just passed a series of laws toughening penalties on drunken driving, and there were no second chances. Virginia is a state that is notoriously tough on crime and true to form they convicted first and asked questions later.

It was on my record as a gross driving misdemeanor and would be there for 10 years. As part of the process, they required attendance at 3 months of treatment and counseling for alcohol and drugs along with mandatory AA meetings. Because I was relocating for work, they required me to find a rehab center in Seattle that was approved by the probation department in Virginia.

The rehab center that was convenient to my house had a 9-month program and the State of Virginia compelled me to complete it, including two AA meetings per week. The penalty for non-compliance was an arrest warrant and one year in jail, even though it was a first offense. I also had no driver's license for one year and had to pay a hefty fine.

My confidence soared though as I had these thoughts. I knew that nothing could stop my meteoric ride to the top. I knew I didn't have a problem with alcohol and would be happy to share that with anyone who cared to listen, including the counselors at the treatment facility. Sure, I liked to party, and yes, I did get pulled over intoxicated, but that happens sometimes, even to great guys like me! I was a social drinker and nothing more.

Upon arrival in Seattle, a taxi took me to a swank three-bedroom corporate apartment that would be my residence for the next three or four months until I either bought a house or rented.

The entire relocation was on the new company's dime, including the rent in this apartment. I was a short two-bus ride from work and a one-bus ride from the treatment center. More importantly, there was a friendly tavern just a block away with some nice people. I decided that this would be my place to spend spare time, getting to know people. The first night in town was my 35th birthday, so I went to this tavern and got wasted, in celebration of a new life, a new town, and a new job, free of the shackles that were left behind in Washington, DC.

Chapter 8

We had a couple of days to settle at the ashram before beginning Sadhana. A Sadhana is a period of practice, or intended spiritual growth. Since we are required to wear traditional Indian dress and nobody owned that style of clothing, we went to town to go shopping. The town is about six kilometers from the ashram and it requires a bus ride or other form of transportation.

Riding a bus in India is a story unto itself. The cost of the bus from the ashram to town is 5 rupees. In today's monetary units that is about 7 U.S. cents. The buses are the largest vehicles on the road. If there are traffic laws in India, they are a very well-kept secret. We recently saw a business in downtown Pondicherry for India Driving School. It wasn't very busy. But much like the harmony of the living beings with nature, the madness of the roadways seemed to work. At any given time, there are bicycles, cycles, scooters, cows, cars, trucks, goats, dogs, pedestrians, ox drawn carts and buses all sharing the same road.

It is intense orderly chaos and there is an ongoing contest to see who can overuse their horn. The buses own the roads. The buses are a microcosm of the traffic patterns, overcrowded and chaotic. So much so that people actually ride the bus either hanging off the side or it, or if really overcrowded, on the roof. Students will sit on the roof of the bus on their way to school. I look forward to one day riding an overcrowded bus while hanging off the side of it!

Downtown most closely resembles a large open air shopping mall, where every building has been turned into a sort of storefront. Goods are sold piecemeal with no consolidation of inventory to one store with the exception of an occasional grocery store that carries multiple food items. Most of the shops are single item stores. So if you need a vacuum cleaner, there is a vacuum cleaner store, and that is all they sell. And right next to it are the only 2 or 3 other vacuum cleaner stores in town.

The downtown area is clogged with scooters, motorcycles and bicycles and people milling around making the economy go. One student was telling me that people in India used to not shop. They waited until they were in almost desperate need of something and then would go out and purchase it. It was a beautiful concept that the culture was based on need rather than want.

Now that the Western version of capitalism is taking hold with the constant barrage of advertising and subliminal messaging appealing to people's egos, making them feel less than for not having certain products, the culture is shifting from the virtue of buying and using what is needed to the Western culture of no virtue based on want. It remains uncertain if the earth can handle the consumption based on wants of another 1.5 billion people, wants that did not exist a mere 20 years ago. It is one of the first virtues that uncontrolled capitalism wipes out in a culture, and that is the virtue of contentment, or being happy with what you have and living a life based on needs rather than wants. It has been said many times that the Earth can support the needs of all, but not the greed of any one man.

The streets were littered with trash, mostly plastic. Prior to plastic arriving on the scene in India, the country was organically eco-friendly. An example of this was the style of eating, a tradition still practiced in many parts of India. People sat on the floor and ate off banana leaves.

There were no utensils used as people ate with their hands. Once the meal was completed, the banana leaf was tossed out the window and a cow would eat it and any leftovers. The sanitation process had yet to catch up to plastic here and the result was piles of trash lining the streets, adding to the clutter of what wealthy capitalists everywhere hoped would be become the world's next 1.5 billion large scale consumer market. I was curious if India would follow the moral decay of other western economies or if this country had the strength to maintain its virtue as it progressed economically.

The room was small with a semi-circle of chairs placed carefully around a flip board with white lesson paper. On the paper read a simple statement: "You are an alcoholic." Five of us sat in the room staring at this message, each one of us telling the sign to go to hell in our own manner. My head was throbbing from my fourth day at the new office and a terrible hangover from the night before. It was one week since my arrival in Seattle, and I had partied every night at the bar near the house. What problem was there? I was at the new job every day at 8:00 am sharp! The pills that had been prescribed to me for anxiety helped quite a bit. I found that the combination of Paxil, a psychotropic drug used to control emotional highs and lows, coupled with Xanax, which I later learned was alcohol in pill form, did wonders to even out the emotions and nerves and allowed me to function normally during the day. I sat in wonder at modern medicine; there was a pill for everything.

The counselor entered the fluorescent lit room and took a seat near the flip board. Ignoring its message, she looked at us down her nose over some very serious looking glasses. She was a middle-aged, thin woman with straw brown hair cut to shoulder length with a needle nose that curved slightly up at the end where the glasses currently perched. She was not in a good mood.

"You are all here because you have broken the law and are criminals in the eyes of society. You are also here because you have a substance abuse problem and are alcoholics and addicts, either to drugs, alcohol or both. You will very shortly be handed an agreement that you will sign and it will be both kept in your file and a copy sent to your probation officer. You will all be here for the next 9 months completing two distinct phases of outpatient drug and alcohol abuse treatment. In addition, you will be required to attend a minimum of two Alcoholics Anonymous or Narcotics Anonymous meetings per week. You will be urine tested randomly for drugs and alcohol and if you fail a urine test or fail to show up for a urine test you will be considered in violation of the treatment program and you will be turned back over to the courts." Her voice was deep for a small framed woman and her lack of a sense of humor was rather appalling. I imagine that she didn't much like her low paying job, and dealing with these criminals every day. She continued, her eyes boring into each of us and judging us as guilty without even a thought to our side of the story:

"Whether you think you are an addict or not is irrelevant. People who are not addicts do not end up here. Each time you introduce yourself you will use your name and say that you are an addict or alcoholic. I can see that each of you has a strong denial in place and you need to overcome this in order for you to recover. You have an opportunity here to change your life, and that choice is yours. If you choose to continue to use drugs and drink you will just end up back here, in the hospital, in jail or dead. Those are the facts. Keep in mind that 19 out of every 20 people in addiction die from it, so this means that 4 of you, if not all 5 of you will die well before your time as a result of your addiction." She finished this sentence with flair, as if she just summed up a thesis for PhD level psychiatry rather than telling a bunch of so-called addicts a lot of information that they didn't want to hear.

I was staring at her hoping to catch her eyes and melt her being with my fury. She had a lot of nerve calling me an addict because of one DUI, much less telling me I was going to die. I was in the prime of my life, on the upswing of the pendulum, and no scrawny low-paid Associates degree woman was going to sit there and talk to me in this manner. In these moments of anger, I could feel it seething out of me, like a sick energy engulfing the area around me.

It felt like raw power that was then forged into my twisted perception of reality.

She pointed a thin finger over to the table on the side of the room. "On that table are cups and urine analysis forms. Please take one of each and provide a urine sample. Also take a clipboard with the contract that you have to sign. Note that if you are taking any prescription drugs, you must list all of them and we will decide if you can continue to take them. Our schedule is 5:30 pm to 9:00 pm Monday to Friday and 8:00 am to noon on Saturday for the first 30 days. Attendance is mandatory. Thereafter, you will attend once a week on a weeknight for eight months. Your probation officer will be given monthly status reports, including the results of all urine tests."

We filed over to get the forms and to pee in a cup. It was incredibly humiliating, but something that I would get used to doing. Once under the boot of the system, it is difficult to get out. I listed the two prescriptions on the contract and gave the form to the counselor. She eyeballed it through the glasses on the end of her nose, looked at me and said "You cannot take Xanax. It is highly addictive and is basically alcohol in pill form. Have you been drinking while taking this?"

My fury was making my hair stand on end and the fist in my left hand was involuntarily clenching. "Who the hell are you to tell me that I can't take a prescription given to me by a doctor for a problem that has nothing to do with why I am here? And what business is it of yours whether I drink while taking it? I can read the damn instructions and don't." This was at the least a stretch of the truth. I didn't take the pill directly with a beer but drank on the drug before it was cleansed from my system. The ability to think had left me and I was in total emotional overdrive. This translated into rage, anger and the inability to make any sense.

"You cannot take the Xanax. Period. I will see about the Paxil. Your problem is not anxiety. You are an alcoholic, and you are using all these substances to try to feel better. You don't have to like it, but it is what you are. And you are here, and while you are here, you will follow the rules, or we will simply kick you out and you can go back to Virginia and spend some time in jail." She finished with a flourish of self-righteousness and walked away.

"Fuck you." I said this flatly, with no punctuation or energy. I walked outside and lit a cigarette, my mind racing with how I could stick it to this place and its dictatorial processes. I had the money and knew from experience that was usually the answer. Maybe my lawyer could get me into a different rehab place, one with an easier and softer approach. I would later find out that this was considered the most difficult rehab clinic in the state, and I had chosen it, mostly out of ignorance.

The probation officer in Virginia had given me a list of approved treatment centers in Seattle and I had just picked the one closest to my apartment to get him off my back. On top of that, had I stayed in Virginia it would only be a three-month program and here I was stuck with nine. The probation officer thought this a good thing given the severity of my offense and the fact that I had apparently miserably failed the drug and alcohol assessment that was given to me prior to moving out West. The system was totally screwed up. Hard core criminals walked out of jailhouses and I was being unfairly and unjustly punished for a first offense driving infraction.

We had to complete the first four steps of the AA program during the duration of the treatment and we were required to get a sponsor in AA. We also had to abstain from any drugs and alcohol. For the first thirty days I abstained. I would later learn that this was called "white-knuckling" because without doing anything other than putting down the bottle, alcoholism gets worse, not better. It was not a good month.

For the first week, my hands were a bit shaky and my nerves were quite on edge. Tempers were short at work and I had immense trouble sleeping. The emotions that surfaced ranged from supreme self-righteousness to feelings of nothingness and lack of self-worth. My anger was set upon anyone that even looked in my general direction and I cursed the God that I didn't believe in for my ill fate. And I ensured that I did nothing, or the very least that I could do to get through the treatment program. I dozed and zoned out during the classes, came to the AA meetings late and left early once my slip was signed and generally just bided my time, steeped in the mountain of denial that I was not an alcoholic.

About two weeks into the program my lawyer called and said that he was having a conversation with the probation officer asking if 30 days was enough given that the program was daily as compared to the one in Virginia, which was weekly. He was basing his argument on the total hours of treatment. This gave me hope. On the last of the 30 days, I stopped in a bar near where the bus changes knowing for certain that my lawyer had convinced the probation officer those thirty days were sufficient. As I drank the first beer, my nerves calmed and my confidence returned. Eight beers and two hours later, I stumbled off the bus at my apartment went to bed, happily knowing that this unhappy phase of my life was over.

At work the next morning my phone rang. It was the alcohol counselor from the treatment center. She informed me that my probation officer called and confirmed that I was in the program for the entire 9 months. I could hear the bemusement in her voice from my end around tactic with my attorney. She enjoyed this. She asked me if I drank last night. I said no, outright lying to her. I would see her Thursday, which was in two days.

I had researched the type of urine tests that were given and most are the variety that if alcohol has not been consumed in a 2 to 3-day window, it will not show positive. I also knew they used a baseline based on the first urine test and was sure that my baseline was a mess, given that I was on Paxil, Xanax and had drank heavily for the 90 plus days leading up to that day.

Given that I had now found my new routine, and that was to control my drinking for the next 8 months. I would drink freely from Thursday evening after group therapy until Monday night, and then stay sober from Tuesday morning until the end of group therapy on Thursday. It was perfect. I guessed correctly that this place was lazy about urine testing and would only test on days that we were in the treatment center. And this was the next 8 months of my life.

Tuesday and Wednesday evenings were a living hell of withdrawal, coupled with a five day weekend of partying, with Saturday and Sunday being all day affairs at the bar. I bought a three bedroom house in the neighborhood across the street from my apartment so that I could remain in walking distance from the bar, had an endless supply of money to support my partying lifestyle, and just had to get through the next eight months without getting caught. Ironically, in October of that year, rehab ended and I got my driver's license back on the same day. The next four years of my life would clarify in my mind the definition of the word hell.

# Chapter 10

Sitting on the floor at the ashram was going to kill me. I was certain of it. We are required to sit on the floor for a minimum of four hours a day in the different classes and practices and for a western body unaccustomed to doing so, it is a torture session. My back is hunched forward at the top of the thoracic spine from sitting at a computer and driving for 25 years, and the major muscle groups in the legs are short and weak from disuse. We learned that anything in the body that is not used atrophies and gets weak. In order for me to sit on the floor, the body required a breaking down and rebuilding of sorts.

My hard, athletic muscles that had been developed from years of ice hockey and volleyball needed to be replaced by lean supple muscles that had both strength and flexibility. My current muscle structure only has strength, and it is unbalanced. As with everything in Yoga including the physical body, balance is sought, and our bodies reflect the unbalance or balance of our lives. And primarily for floor sitting, the hip flexors and muscles on the front sides of the hips needed to be built from scratch.

In addition, my hunched back and spine needed to be lengthened and straightened before any attempt at sitting comfortably on the floor could be attained. In order to access all the higher practices in yoga, including Pranayama and all the concentration or meditative practices, it is necessary to be able to sit comfortably. It is impossible to be comfortable if the body is screaming in agony and sending pain and discomfort signals to the brain.

This was going to be a process, so as I sat, I started to lift my heart to straighten the spine and relax my knees to the earth. Each time I did this, either the hips, knees or spinus erectus muscles screamed out in agony. It was quite a spectacle. I came to name the classes beginning, intermediate and advanced floor sitting depending on the amount of time we were required to sit on the floor and how much we had sat on the floor that day prior to the current class. Usually by the end of the day all the classes were advanced floor sitting. And that was just sitting on the floor with the legs crossed in a posture called Sukha Asana, which means easy posture. I found that amusing, given that there was nothing *easy* about it.

We also had to learn to sit in a posture called Vajra Asana for long periods of time, which was on the knees, hips to heels. This posture stretched the front sides of the ankles and was painful to the shoelace part of the foot, the ankles and the knees. One was no better than the other. I became aware of something as time passed at the ashram, and that was of a process occurring within me.

When I came to the ashram, I had broken down my mind and emotions through the program of Alcoholics Anonymous, and rebuilt myself. The body, however, was not broken down and rebuilt. AA doesn't focus in this physical realm, only in the physical realm of relationships with self and other human beings. I realized that in order for me to be a complete human being, this process had to occur; I had to break down the body and start anew. I had to pick up the pieces and put myself back together in the physical realm. And since everything is attached to everything, the mind and emotions would come along for the ride.

As the first two months crawled by there was a rhythm developing in my systems, and it was a clear rhythm of detoxification. It would start with pain in the joints and muscles as the body adjusted to sitting on the floor and the posture straightened after years of slumping. In addition, sitting and sleeping on the hard surfaces was breaking down the other muscles in the body and making them suppler. This went on for about a week, and then the body would begin to itch from neck to toes. It would start off mild and turn into a raging fire, like red ants were eating through my skin from the inside out. This would usually last for about four hours followed by extreme sweating and then three days of diarrhea. The cycle would repeat itself three times in the first two months at the ashram.

Sometimes at the end of the day in Satsang, the pain in the back or knees would be so excruciating that it would cause tears of pain. I would sit paralyzed in pain unable to lift my head. There was no movement to make it stop short of standing, which I could not do.

I would sit looking at the floor, slowly rocking from back and forth or from side to side, trying to ease the messages from the back to the pain center in the brain. I would send energy to the space, breathing into it, repeating over and over to myself that this was a process; it was part of my *Tapas* or discipline, to grow. In the long run, this was going to prevent difficulties when I was older, and allow me to beautifully access the higher practices. It was necessary; otherwise the universe would not have put me here.

One day I was passing the Guru and I respectfully bowed my head with hands at heart center. We are to never pass the Guru without showing respect for them and the Yoga lineage. The Guru smiled at me and I could feel his gentle eyes sending me compassion. He knew what I was going through, and had seen it before. If I was in any danger of hurting myself, they would have corrected my practice, but they knew it was good for me, albeit not pleasant.

This concept is a key teaching; as a Yogi; we must learn to do well, and not always what is pleasant, and there is a difference. And pain is often the touchstone of growth. The Guru stopped me and placed his hand on my shoulder, sending a wave of peaceful energy through me.

"I hear you have been having some physical difficulties." I returned his gaze and smiled. I had already been through the *Tapas* of hell, and knew the growth that stemmed from it.

"Yes Guruji. Quite a few. But it is worth the growth on the other side." He smiled and continued on his way. I smiled and walked on, and wondered to myself if I believed what I said.

It was 3:00 in the afternoon on a Wednesday and my hands were shaking terribly. The cigarette trembled uncontrollably as I brought it to my lips for a drag. Fortunately, not too many people were at the bar today; it usually didn't get busy for happy hour until after four. I had a cold beer in front of me and was wondering how I could pick it up and drink it without spilling it all over the place. Maybe I should order a shot first to calm my nerves. Maybe I should have stopped at home first and had a couple beers before coming here.

Alcoholism had me in its death grip, and I fought with that reality each day. I had no idea how I was still holding a job. I would show up to work 1-2 hours late, hung-over and shaky, lock myself in my office avoiding any personal contact, and pretend to answer email. Sometimes at lunch the cravings would get so bad that I would sneak home and have a glass of wine to settle my nerves or stop at one of the local bars for a beer.

Sometimes I could make it through lunch but would have to leave by 3:00 pm at the latest to the get to the bar. The mind was completely obsessed with alcohol, twenty four hours a day, either suffering from the effects of the previous evening or obsessing about how I could get a drink in me. Guilt and shame would shift to self-righteous anger to self-pity. Hiding behind the justification that it was my right to drink when, where and how much I wanted was killing me and that was the hill of denial I was willing to stand and die on. I was a superhero and a nothing all at once, confused about why no other thoughts would enter my mind.

I was a hopeless drunk and was in complete control at the same time. But most of all, there was pain. A pain so deep and unyielding that it had no source, no beginning, and no end. It stretched like a drum over my sanity and when I tried to penetrate it the reverberation sent me back to the bottle. Sometimes I wished that I could stop but knew that I couldn't. Sometimes I wished that I could drink myself to oblivion and that one day I wouldn't awaken. Acceptance was settling in that this was my fate, and I was hoping I could keep the job long enough until whatever end there was.

Otherwise, it would be difficult to pay for this habit for long. For a while, this fear had been driving me to show up to work just enough to stay employed, but I was unsure of how long I could hold out. It would be prophetic that in a few months I would "voluntarily" leave the company even though I was being managed out for being ineffective. My life had progressively become a blur of drunkenness, followed by a blur of trying to get through the day so that I could drink. The physical manifestations of the disease were starting to take control as my hands shook uncontrollably without alcohol and I couldn't think of anything but drinking 24 hours a day. And while I didn't know any of this at the time, I had slipped into late stage alcoholism, the results of which are almost always fatal.

People that used to come up to me in the bar for a laugh or to share a story now avoided me. They looked at me with a sad and confused look, the same look I saw in myself in the mirror. I was losing weight and my abdomen was sore. I had begun to lose the hair on my body due to vitamin deficiency. As these thoughts crossed my mind, I ordered a shot and a beer. There was nothing that could be done about it today, so into oblivion I went.

# Chapter 12

The Guru was quite clear on the cleansing plan that we practiced for the first two months. They had been teaching this regimen for 40 years and it was the preferred method for spiritual growth. "We break down the mind, body and emotions with a series of practices, and then look at the pieces and see what we want to pick up and keep. The remainder we discard as it is no longer a part of who we are. Our spiritual life should be this constant process of self-review, or **Swadiyaya**, breaking ourselves down into pieces and then building back up, with periods of rest in between. The spiritual path is not linear; it is a series of concentric circles leading upward in a conical shape."

He was wearing the usual orange khurta, no shirt and a matching sari across the shoulders. He was explaining to us the process of Shanka Prakshala, a cleansing of the gastro-intestinal tract. "We will cleanse the digestive tract from the mouth to the anus. This will give us an interesting realization of the connection between the two.

The technique involves drinking salt water with a salt content no higher than the normal salt content of the body and then quickly moving the body through the digestive system with a series of Yoga Kriyas. The quick movement of the salt water, the compression in the digestive system, and the abrasiveness of the salt will cleanse the digestive system. The salt will then act as a healing agent for any light abrasions in the small intestines caused by the cleaning. We will continue to drink the salt water and move it through the system two glasses at a time until the discharge from the anus is clear.

43

You may continue for a few more cups after that to be thorough but that is your choice." He finished with his piercing but gentle eyes studying the reaction from each of us. Satisfied that he had made his point clearly he asked if there were any questions. Hope, the youngest of the students, had been having major issues with constipation, much like me, and jumped in. "How many glasses does it take?" She was local to Southern India in nearby Chennai, and had a beautiful smile and a perky attitude.

As was common with women from India, she had long black hair that was worn in many combinations including braiding and multiple types of ponytails. Oftentimes, there were fresh flowers in her hair as Southern India seemed to always be in bloom with a variety of flowers. Today she had a simple ponytail running long down her back with a small white flower pinned to the side of her hair. Her deep brown eyes always smiled and glistened when she spoke. She had a beautiful outward energy that projected love and care that never seemed to turn off. Although with this question, there was a hint of fear in her voice because of her digestive issues.

"It depends," the Guru said flatly. "I have practiced many times and can clean the system with 6 cups of water in 15 minutes. If a student is having constipation issues, it may take over 25 cups of water. The average is 12 to 16. Do not worry yourselves, this is a safe and beautiful practice and many students with chronic digestive issues have completed this and found that their digestive issues were completely resolved. It is more than just the physical cleansing. The awareness that we develop also allows us to let go of many emotional traumas associated with digestion.

You will all be assigned your own bathroom and when you have to go, you just stop where you are and go. Then when you get back, start where you left off." The Guru instilled confidence when he spoke, energy was transmitted that assured us that everything was going to be OK. Alicia, a student from Costa Rica, had the next question.  She was in her early fifties and in incredible physical condition.  She was disciplined physically and mentally and was strong from overcoming a difficult childhood.  She had been teaching Yoga for some time and since English was a second language, she spoke slowly and carefully, with a thick accent.

"You mention that the salt water may cause slight damage to the intestines.  How quickly will that heal?  Is there any danger?"  She was brave and I sensed that she was asking the question more for Hope that for herself.  She had thin, strong facial structure that gave way to beauty once the surface was scratched.  I imagined that she had not had an easy life and was used to having a wall around her emotions.

"We will be fasting for 3 days from the time of the cleansing. Water only and then fruit only on the fourth day.  This will give the body time to heal.  Fasting is a beautiful practice of **Tapas** (discipline) and also allows us to realize that we can survive without food for up to 21 days, sometimes more.  We get energy from the sun and from our breath.  When we fast, we actually begin to control the survival instinct.  This is of profound importance to our spiritual growth.  The survival instinct is one of the oldest instincts in our brain, and while it is obviously necessary, it is often in control when it doesn't need to be.  Look at any situation where there is a mob mentality, and you see a collective survival instinct in play."

At that point he finished the conversation for the evening saying that he would answer any additional questions while we were performing the practice with us the following morning.  We were also informed that we would be completing a coffee enema the last morning of our fast in order to further cleanse the large intestines. There was some cringing among the students at this mention, and I smiled, having prepared by practicing enema at home during a juice cleanse a week prior to arrival.

The popcorn ceiling was starting to stain an obnoxious yellow from all the smoking.  The spot on the directly above was a dark ocher which had non-symmetric rings moving outward in lighter shades of yellow.  This was the view when I first opened my eyes each morning, and it reminded me of the disease that was spreading within me, permeating from my core, spreading outward and slowly killing me.  At this point I welcomed it and wished the core would expand quicker.  At the same time, it pained me to know that the house I was in, the house I bought and had owned for three years, was in foreclosure.

In fact, I was fairly certain that the bank was about two weeks from taking it away.  This would most likely cause me to end up either in a shelter or on the street, as I hadn't worked in two years and unemployment was running out.  I cursed the bank, the job market and a God I didn't believe in for my situation.  Self-hatred welled up inside from my deepest being and I took that hatred and pointed it squarely at the world for putting me in this predicament.

I rolled over to the right side, noticing how filthy the sheets were from the combination of sweat, spilled beer and wine, cigarette ashes and the lack of washing them for two months.  It is difficult to wash laundry when the city has turned off the water.  I grabbed a cigarette and lit it, inhaling the poisoned smoke deeply and holding it in as if to make a point.  On the exhale I noticed how it hit the center of the dark spot on the ceiling and then spread outward, dissipating into the broken energy of the room, dissipating like my life force.  I smoke because I chose to do so.  Nobody was in the room or the house to make the point to so I made it to myself, the self-righteous ego in complete control. I began going through the list of people and institutions that had wronged me and brought me to this point of existence. There was the last company where I worked and earned quite a bit of salary.

They had deemed me unnecessary in reorganization, and while they had given me the opportunity to find another role in the company, it was a losing battle. I was deemed a weak performer and nobody would hire me, particularly at my pay scale. My boss was a jackass for allowing my review to be worded that poorly, poisoning any chance that I had for growth. I pointed a lot of hatred in that direction. The city was next on the list; how was I supposed to do laundry and have water to drink if they turned the water off? Couldn't they see that I was temporarily having a setback? I knew I had to get up at some point today and walk down to the convenience store with my gallon jugs and take water from their bathroom. This was also a major inconvenience and it worried me what the neighbors thought. I feared even leaving the house.

At least the power was on, for now. I hadn't paid the bill and I was certain that at some point they would come by and turn it off. Later today I would spend a fair amount of time on the couch looking out the window in fear of the utility truck coming by to turn off my power. I lit another cigarette and flipped on the TV.

Ah, no cable. I would have to watch DVDs today. I began to think about how I would get even with everyone and everything that had brought me to this point and it occurred to me that I was thirsty. I went downstairs in my underwear, 5 days of growth on my face, and poured myself a glass of red wine from the bottle that I hadn't finished last night. The clock in the kitchen read 8:45 am. I looked at the glass of wine and my soul cried out in anguish.

Self-pity turned to anger and then despair in seconds. I had been through the emotional cycle so many times that the world had just started to grey out.  For about a month I had promised myself that today was the day that I would not drink, I would take it one day at a time and not drink, like I had heard in AA meetings four years prior.  The next I knew I would be baffled and drunk by 9:30 am, unable to understand why.  The world had greyed out to a point where I had given up and was just drinking on borrowed time until death took me.

I welcomed the thought.  But a different part of me I didn't know and would not know for some time was screaming from the mountain tops to stop, to just please for the sake of all that is good in the world to please stop.  Just once, don't take that drink.  In this state of spiritual bankruptcy, I didn't hear that voice.  I felt the guilt of being me, the shame of being alive and the embarrassment of what people now saw in me.  I hated all that was, is and will be but this time I pointed the hatred inward.

My soul wept, empathetically trying to reach out a hand to my heart and mind.  But the mind was too far gone, the heart shattered in the morass of self-pity.  Alcohol was my master, I was its slave, and I just wished that before my final breath someone would please explain to me what the hell was wrong with me.  The wine passed over my lips and another day of oblivion began.  I would drink 2 bottles of wine and 18 beers that day, in the prison of my own home, in the prison of my own mind.  This oblivion lasted for 550 days, almost two full years.

# Chapter 14

We had just completed fasting and our coffee enema and were informed that it was time to begin the cleansing of the nervous system. The salt water cleanse had gone about average for me, taking 12 glasses of water to first start excretion and then another 4 to complete the process with clear excretion.

The nervous system cleansing was a Pranayama technique that worked against the natural biorhythm of the body in the primary nerves that ran up the spine. The technique allowed for a deep understanding of the subconscious, a dredging like a ship dredges the bottom of the ocean, searching for past experiences that are still controlling the behaviors but are buried in the subconscious.

By gaining awareness of these subconscious patterns, we can dispose of them, cleansing our nervous system of past traumas. It sounded like a wild roller coaster ride, and I had some serious doubts to its feasibility. This would be the final practice in our first two months of breaking down and it would take two weeks of daily practice to complete. We would complete it as part of our daily Pranayama session.

Sitting in **Satsangha** the evening before we were to begin the nervous system cleansing, the Guru was informing us of the process. "You may experience emotions that don't fit in the framework of where you are in any given moment. Sometimes, these emotions may have a direct cause that you can see and link, an event in your past. Others you may have no link, just the intensity of the emotion or series of emotions.

These may arise during the practice itself, after the practice or even in your dreams. The key to succeeding in this practice is having intention and the awareness of what is happening which is why the ashram environment is a perfect setting for the practice. The isolation from the outside world helps to minimize the number of mental distractions allowing for additional clarity in thought." The Guru was in a zone and his voice was beautifully reassuring and soothing.

Dredging through the skeletons in one's closet is not a comfortable exercise for some, especially when those skeletons have been locked in the subconscious. The beauty of the human body and its superior design did however have a protection mechanism built in. Our subconscious mind would not show us anything we were not ready to see. The Guru continued, his hand waving back and forth in front of him, hypnotizing us to the rhythm of the natural cadence of his voice. "If something arises during the practice itself, stop the breathing exercise and come into a squat position (Utkata Asana) with the hands fully touching the Earth (Spasha Mudra) to release the energy of the emotion and then pick up where you left off in the practice.

Try to remember if there is any association with the emotion and journal it immediately after the practice for further contemplation. If something arises outside of the practice but during waking hours, carry a journal with you so that you can track it for contemplation. Take a moment, if possible to focus on the emotion and the associated past event, if feasible. And if in a dream, journal the dream immediately upon waking. My experience with the dream process in this practice is that the dreams are quite vivid and there have been other students who have been light or non-dreamers who have reported consistent and vivid dreams during this practice. The effects of the practice will last for up to 80 days after we complete the 11$^{th}$ day, but will lessen with time.

You are encouraged to repeat the practice quarterly as it usually takes about 3 to 4 years of a consistent practice to completely cleanse the nervous system. We should keep in mind that the nervous system carries our entire emotional trauma from when we were inside the mother's womb all the way to the present moment and that it is carried and remembered at the cellular level. Our subconscious remembers everything, including every commercial we have seen, every movie we have viewed and every event we have witnessed, actively or passively. This is why it is important to not discount anything." The Guru finished the statement with a flourish and fell silent. There was a sense that there would be no questions tonight as he brought his hands to Namaskar signaling it was time to Om and end the evening.

It was below freezing and a thin layer of ice was forming on the tops of the grass blades from the moisture in the air. The driveway was slippery and half frozen and my car just sat there motionless, staring at me, daring me to get behind the wheel. It had been idle for six months as I was not allowed to drive for a rather gross example of driving under the influence of alcohol, my second such offense. My court date for that infraction had been two days earlier, and it was impressed upon me that I was going to jail for one to five years unless I entered into a deferred prosecution program. This is a program where an individual admits that they have an addiction to drugs or are alcoholic, and then become a ward of the state for five years.

The first two years is mandatory substance abuse treatment and multiple support group meetings each week. In addition, there are monthly meetings with a probation officer as well as random urine tests to ensure that sobriety is maintained. That is then followed by three years of unsupervised probation. If the program is completed, the charges are dropped. Failure to complete the program or getting new charges while in the program means that the individual is responsible for the original charges and the new charges, if any.

The reason the state was taking such a dim view of my arrest was the particular veracity of the level of alcohol in my blood which was measured at 0.29, more than 3 times the legal limit. For most people, this amount of alcohol in the bloodstream requires hospitalization. I was also driving on a Sunday afternoon in this condition, which is equally disturbing. If this had been a first offense, there may have been some wiggle room, but it was my second in four years, the first one being in a different state.

I pondered this as a walked back from the courthouse two days prior. I knew that it wasn't enough to keep me sober. I had been arrested a total of four times over my drinking career and the laws of man were not an inhibitor to my drinking or the way I drank. I could not control at any point in my life the amount I drank and this continually baffled me.

Self-promise after self-promise of just one or two drinks turned into six or ten drinks followed by justifications that it was OK, followed by thinking it was normal, followed by maybe thinking that it was abnormal but finding people who drank the same way so it became normal, followed by guilt and embarrassment by the way I drank, followed by isolated drinking, followed by not caring and drinking for oblivion. Hospitalization was also not an inhibitor to my drinking as I had been hospitalized on three separate occasions for either withdrawal, excessive intake of alcohol or injuries related to being drunk.

For the past 550 or so days prior to showing up for court, I was drinking for destruction. I was drinking for the sickest reason of all, oblivion and death, and it was a conscious decision. The subconscious is a funny thing. I noticed that when I was trying to live and be "better" my subconscious would try to pull me down. It is the survival instinct of the ego. When I was actively trying to kill myself, the ego tried to save me. Same survival instinct, differently applied. The end result was the same though: unresolved internal conflict.

I thought diligently about life during this walk home. I was drunk because I had needed a six pack of beer before going to court that day. My thoughts were completely addled but somewhere on that walk I had a moment of clarity, however brief. But beyond a moment of clarity, it was a moment of hope.

53

Hopelessness had gripped my soul for so long that this feeling of hope was foreign. It marched into my heart and for a brief second I felt better, and it moved from my heart to my mind, where my mind, in this moment of clarity, thought that maybe this life *was* worth living, even though the current state of it was a complete shamble. It occurred to me somewhere beyond any part of my mind that I recognized that I should have gratitude for the life I was given, and that it might be possible to live without alcohol.

This moment of clarity was the final tipping point; I either made the decision to live, or I stopped on the way home and picked up another case of beer and continued into oblivion, which surely meant death. My body was down to 145 pounds, 45 pounds under my normal weight. I couldn't be sure, but I thought I was dying from malnutrition. The hair on my body had stopped growing and my legs looked like they were shaven, except badly with a dull razor, with intermittent bald spots.

I didn't remember the last time I had eaten anything of substance. Every once in a while I stopped at a sub shop and got a small sub and some chips if I had money left over from buying cigarettes, alcohol and dog food. Eating occurred about every three or four days. I kept telling myself things could be worse. The unemployment checks that were supporting my habit kept coming due to the ongoing recession. I still had the house, although it was in foreclosure. These thin threads were what I had held onto to prove to myself that I was not an alcoholic, but these threads were starting to fray, like the nerves of my existence, and one or the other was going to snap.

I felt more than just sick physically. The spirit and will to live had left, sucked out of me in a perverse throng of irrational fears eating at my existence and ruling my thoughts and actions like a relentless slave driver, his whip beating and scarring my soul. But was this who I was? It was certainly who I had become. But if I had become this over time, then certainly I could un-become it. Through the emotional bankruptcy, the searing irrationality of the mind and my own twisted perception of the world in which I lived, somehow a decision was made. I stopped drinking that day.

Two days later suffering from severe alcohol withdrawal known as delirium tremens and hallucinating in the freezing cold weather, I stood there in shorts with no shirt, emaciated from malnutrition, hopping from bush to bush outside my house trying to find my ex-fiancée.

I was certain she was in one of the bushes as her face kept appearing in them, rotating from bush to bush. The same ex-fiancée that now lived 2,500 miles away in the bushes in the front of my house. She looked very disappointed in me as she appeared and disappeared. As I stood there howling and yelling at my shrubbery and hopping around in the sub-freezing February evening with that almost frozen grass crunching under my feet, I felt a sense of something happening in one of the recesses of my mind. There was a decision being made about my life and its direction, but my conscious mind was not a part of it. There was a brief vision of my beaten body lying naked in a filthy bathtub and a white cat circling the tub. I was trying to talk, to no one. I looked dead.

Flashing lights added to the state of confusion as the police had arrived. They approached me carefully to see if I was armed, and seeing that I wasn't, asked me if I was taking any drugs or on substances. I told them that my ex-fiancée who lived in Washington, DC was hiding in all my shrubs and that my neighbor behind me had wired my house and was listening to all my conversations that I had when I was home alone. He was a spy, of this I was sure. I somehow worked in that I had quit drinking a couple days earlier. Something very strange happened. The officer sat me down on my front porch and put a blanket around me. He told me that an ambulance was coming and that I was going to be helped. For a brief moment, I felt compassion from another human being. It was a new emotion for me.

Thirty minutes later in the hospital the medical team assigned to me had run a series of blood tests and an EKG for the heart. They were frantically sticking needles into me with bags attached to them and the doctor kept saying 'in the nick of time'. I would later be informed that in my advanced state of malnutrition I had about two days left to live. My heart was about to seize from potassium deficiency.

Potassium is a key component in electrical process of the heartbeat. My life had been spared, for reasons that were completely beyond my understanding. The universe would smile on me again about 30 days later with the sale of my home just prior to the bank officially taking it, making me homeless. I would lose $200,000 on the sale, and that, coupled with the $150,000 that I spent from savings and retirement accounts on drinking and partying, made me officially broke. I received just enough cash from the sale to get a small apartment down the street. It also occurred to me on this walk home that I had done some terrible things, and treated people that loved me very poorly, mostly by being unavailable. My family lived 2,500 miles away and while they had some idea of what was going on, they did not know the depths of my despair.

## Part Two

## *Believe in Something, and Then Take the First Step... ...*

# Chapter 16

Day one of the Pranayama practice to cleanse the nervous system was over. The actual practice had lasted five minutes since it was only one cycle of breathing on the first day. I felt nothing, and my old habit of instant gratification kicked in telling me that this practice was a hoax, it wouldn't work for me! As I left the practice area and wandered out into the sun, it seemed that my mind began to bend in upon itself. Space twisted into a time lapse and the sun became shards of light sprinkling down around me. The sense of touch was distant, and a shroud settled over the mind, but not the shroud of confusion as was my past experience.

This shroud shielded me from the illusion that was day to day life and began to show me the levels below, but from such a safe distance that objectivity and discernment were present. It felt like watching a film, only I was the star, and from this distance, I could be detached from the outcome of the movie. There was no hero to root for, no villain to shun, only the learning experience of the event itself, unblemished by my own sensory perception, undiluted by my likes and dislikes, and unfiltered from my ego. I watched these events as if in a balloon floating above.

*7 Years Prior.* On about my third beer, JR walked into the bar. He was a squat man, pencil thin mustache, always had a hat on with the name of a different brand of construction equipment. Blue jeans were the outfit of choice with a flannel shirt, opened to reveal a firm beer gut and a t-shirt with a message. Today's read, "Guns don't kill people, people kill people." I was on my third beer and we started chatting. He started telling me a story about a bitch ex-wife, credit card debt and an aggressive lawyer that wanted to garnish his wages.

It was odd but he really seemed in a bad way about this so I asked him how much. He said he needed $3,000, desperately. For some reason I agreed to lend it to him.

Deep inside me a voice was telling me this was a bad idea, but deeper inside me was a feeling that this needed to be done. I felt intuitively that this money was gone, but even with that intuition the deeper being in me said to do it anyway. I did it, my ego telling me that everyone would think I was a great guy for helping a friend out of a scrape. Later I found out that everyone thought I was an idiot. Two months later JR and his wife skipped town to Jacksonville, FL to escape their cocaine dealer whom they owed a considerable amount of money.

A soft voice came to my perception, recognizable as my teacher within:

*"JR left an oyster knife at our house after a party, thus it became known as the $3,000 oyster knife. It is one of a kind! The oyster knife is very special to us, even though we haven't used it since. It reminds us that we should be grateful to be alive. The last time we were hospitalized with delirium tremens, the doctor told us we had about two days left to live. Had we an extra $3,000 to spend on booze and cigarettes, we would have certainly died.*

*Sometimes we cannot immediately see the universe at work in our lives, and the cause and effect of every situation. This is Karma. We must realize that the Universe has been working for us in our life and the karma of the universe has been working in our life long before we got sober, we were just not able to see it and piece it together. In this case we made a very poor decision (to loan a known drug addict money), which was god karma on our part, he didn't repay the money; bad karma on his part. This event was a major contributing factor to our life being saved from our path of destruction. This realization is a beautiful spiritual lesson of cause and effect. The famous*

*Czechoslovakian writer Vaclav says that 'true faith is not knowing that everything will be OK, but the certainty that everything will eventually make sense. Try to remember this.'*

**40 Years Prior.** On a suburban street lined with ranch style houses and nicely manicured lawns, I see myself walking home from school. It is a clear, late fall day and the leaves are unable to make up their mind on a resting place as the wind tosses them from the street to the sidewalk and then back to the lawn where the owner of the home will have to diligently rake them back to the street for pickup. I notice that the child that is me is walking funny and picking at his hind end and has to use the bathroom. Even though it just around the block to our house and a very short walk, it seems I cannot wait. In a panic the child darts up to a door asking to use a neighbor's bathroom. I look about 8 or 9 years old and am an innocent child, so of course they allow us to use the bathroom. The boy is so sick that the toilet won't flush. Mortified, I sneak out of the house and run home. Guilt, shame and embarrassment consume me for days, and I even walk to school the longer way around the other block for weeks.

The soft voice inside is now filled with compassion, and this compassion is transmitted to my heart. I feel an immediate release in my entire being as the voice speaks.

*"We must let go of the guilt and shame of childhood that should have never been there in the first place. We did nothing wrong, we were a sick child that was about to have an accident. We must let this go."*

**39 Years Prior.** A child sits daydreaming staring out the first floor window of a suburban school. He is 9 years old with light brown hair, parted on the left and straight. The boy is average height but gives off an intense sensitivity to the world. He jitters and cannot sit still, squeamishly and unconsciously shifting his weight from side to side. His brown eyes might be lost in thoughts of street hockey or

60

playing on the jungle gym about 100 yards across freshly cut grass on the blacktop playground. The boy feels. Everything.

It is like the amplifier of his senses and intuition is turned up too high, and he doesn't know how to turn it down, or how to explain the feeling. He feels abnormal and constantly questions whether he belongs. He is an outsider looking in and doesn't understand why. The daydreams take him away from the discomfort. It is the only coping mechanism he has learned in his young life. The noon recess bell rings and all the students file out to play in the grass and on the playground. Recess was always a good time for the boy, playing took him away from the feelings. Playing games, sports, it didn't matter; it was an escape that was acceptable both to him and the other students.

The boy was both smart and athletic, but shy and afraid. This kept him from being who he really was, fear of the unknown but very real suppressing him at every turn. The winter in upstate NY had been particularly brutal that year and the spring was a welcome sign. The pollen from the plants was potent and the boy had terrible allergies and hay fever. At this time, there was no over the counter allergy medicine as seasonal allergies were not well understood and only handled by specialists. Each time the boy came in from recess in the spring, a session of uncontrollable sneezing coupled with bloodshot and watery eyes that got so puffy that they closed sometimes. The boy also couldn't breathe from his nose. The other students laughed at him, always.

One day the teacher asked the boy what was causing the allergy. The boy did not know. He was afraid to answer because he did not know. He was embarrassed to answer because he would be laughed at some more. All he felt were guilt and shame for having the allergies.

Prior to recess the following day the teacher brought a bundle of dandelions in and put them on the boy's desk. She left them there for 30 minutes until the boy's eyes swelled shut and his nose started running. The other students laughed at the boy some more and the teacher said "See, you are allergic to dandelions."

*"We must let go and understand that children don't know better. Adults like this should, but sometimes don't. We must forgive, in this respect."*

**Current Day.**

"Sarvesh. Sarvesh?" I heard this voice repeating my name. "Are you OK?" It was Hope and she was giggling. I snapped out of it and looked at her, confusion spreading across my face. It seemed to me as if time had warped and I wasn't in the right place or moment. "We are done with the nervous system cleansing!! All eleven days, and it is our off day!!" She bounded out of the practice room for breakfast. I just sat there, mummified. Where had the last 11 days gone?

If I had been given a new lease on life, it sure didn't feel like it. There is a common misconception that when an alcoholic quits drinking, their life gets better. This was my thought process when I quit drinking, especially after the doctors at the hospital pumped me full of delicious nutrients that I had starved from my body for close to two years.

I actually felt great, for about a week. And I also immediately stopped getting arrested and hospitalized, which I suppose is better. But then I experienced what alcoholism *really* is, and it was something that would take me another year to fully understand.

In order to understand alcoholism, we need to understand that alcohol is not *really* the problem. And this sounds very odd to both the alcoholic, and to the people trying to help the alcoholic. So in a lot of cases, nobody really has any idea what is going on. Simply put, if alcohol was the problem, we would just quit drinking and all go merrily on our way. When an alcoholic quits drinking, the disease gets worse, if left untreated. Using Alcohol is but a symptom of the disease, and the substance used to control the emotions and problems created by the disease.

Once the alcoholic quits drinking, the coping mechanism has been removed. The demons return, the rubber band begins to tighten, and there is no outlet to resolve the massive internal mental conflicts driven by the thousand forms of fear and the twisted perception of the world that the alcoholic has developed. There are really only two questions that any alcoholic needs to answer to identify if they are indeed suffering from the disease of alcoholism.

First, can they stop drinking on their own?  Second, when they start drinking, can they control the amount that they drink?  If they answer 'no' to both of those questions, they are most likely alcoholic.

I was trying to wrap my head around this as it was explained to me by our counselor in the rehab facility.  This time I chose a much friendlier rehab facility, and even though this time was also under the thumb of the law, I was there to recover, rather than to continue my drinking career.

There was a small part of me that was still holding out that I could drink normally again, the folly of every alcoholic, and I was terrified of figuring out how to live a life without booze, but at this point it was better than the alternative.  That hope and smidgen of willingness that had allowed me to quit in the first place was still there, gently flickering like a candle in an ocean breeze.  Sometimes it felt as if it would die out, but just when I thought it would, the wind would die down just enough to allow the light to remain.

I could faintly hear my soul begging and pleading with me daily, hourly even, to stick it out, that it was going to all be worth it.  I was highly skeptical.  At least I was working again.  I had found a job doing what I had done 17 years prior and for about the same inflation-adjusted pay.  That gave me hope too, because in my previous state I was unemployable.

The alcohol and substance abuse treatment schedule was five days a week for two months, one day a week for ten months and one day a month for one year.  I was also required to attend two AA meetings per week and have a court slip signed that was reviewed by my probation officer and the treatment center.  I had a Breathalyzer in my car and was allowed to drive under that condition only.  The Breathalyzer is a device installed in a vehicle to ensure that the driver of the vehicle has not been drinking and the device will not allow the car to start until the driver breathes into it with no alcohol on the breath.

The total cost of this was north of $20,000, and is now considered the most expensive bar tab I have ever had. I had nothing as my drinking had caused total financial ruin. The house sold at the peak of the recession for a $200,000 loss. I drank $150,000 in savings, stock and retirement accounts before the house went into foreclosure during the 550-day bender. And while all that was bad enough, what really ate at me was that I more or less wasted an entire decade of my life, my thirties, inside a bottle, having gained sobriety three months after my 40th birthday. I sat in rehab pondering the absurdity that my life was during the recent past and the absurdity it had become and seriously questioned why I was given the opportunity to live.

A large serving of humble pie, topped with guilt, shame and embarrassment was being served to me by the universe on a daily basis. I sat judging myself the same way that I had always judged myself, by my job, my income and my belongings. I had none of the above so I felt like a nothing. I was about to learn that my entire belief system of what made up a human being was drastically and profoundly wrong, and that my value system was twisted like my perception after a night of vodka.

This belief system would all need to be razed to the ground and rebuilt anew, if I wanted to live a happy life, and not a life built on materialism or the perception of materialism, but a life that had a foundation of virtue that would provide the happiness that I sought. But I first needed to begin taking responsibility for my actions, and this meant getting sober and doing whatever it took to stay sober. We are asked if we are willing to go to any length to stay sober, and for at least today, my answer was yes. My hope was that I could still answer yes to that question tomorrow, next week, next month and next year.

Chapter 18

Every month at the ashram we are given a Karma Yoga duty to perform which is work that we do to support the ashram and to give freely of our time with the expectation of nothing in return. It is a nice lesson in this day and age of "What is in it for me?" Karma Yoga is considered one of the paths to enlightenment and it is the altruistic offering of service to others asking nothing in return. During the second month me and one of the other students, Rahan, were put on janitor duty. This meant we had to clean the bathrooms and sweep out the Pranayama practice space each day.

The hut where we practiced Pranayama collected caterpillar feces from the inhabitants of the coconut leaf roof. To make cleaning the toilets more amusing, Rahan and I started a fictional company and took after Indian culture by naming it after one of the Hindu Gods, or in this case Goddesses. Lackshmi is the Goddess of Wealth and Plentifulness, and so the Lackshmi Janitorial Company was born. From this we spawned an empire of Lackshmi companies, based on whatever odd jobs we were asked to complete at the ashram. We had the Lackshmi dining services company for when we were asked to serve meals, the Lackshmi pest control company for when we needed to remove rats from one of the spare rooms and so on. It was a lot of fun and it gave us something to do while the rain pounded away at us.

During janitorial services, it had been raining for five weeks straight and there didn't appear to be an end in sight. We were all wet, cold and taking turns being sick. The open air rooms were great when it was sunny, or even hot, but with the high humidity and constant moisture, everything we owned was damp, mildew, moldy or all of the above. Our clothing was starting to smell. When it rains during monsoon season in India, it rains hard all day and night and it is not uncommon for five or six inches of rain to fall in one day. There was a stationary low pressure front sitting off the coast on the ocean spinning in a circle and it wasn't moving. It just picked the water up out of the ocean and dumped it on the shore.

The streets were getting flooded, the sewer systems, which ran back into the ocean, were at a breaking point and different parts of the town were underwater. It turns out that this was the worst monsoon season that southern India has seen in 30 years. The mood of the students, and even the teachers, was glum, and tempers were starting to flair. One of the students blew up at breakfast because he thought the student that was serving him was shortchanging his portions. We are overfed at the ashram, so this attitude was preposterous, yet understandable given the decline in living conditions during the deluge of rain.

I took it upon myself to boost morale and wrote this on the whiteboard in the kitchen one morning.

---

**_Weather forecast from God:_**

-Rain for 40 days and 40 nights.

**Further Instructions**

-Build one large ark

-Gather one male and one female of each animal species

-If you don't make it on the ark, please learn to swim

"We apologize for any inconvenience that the weather is causing, if you would like to file a complaint, please reach out to us using normal prayer channels and we will get back to you as soon as an angel is available to call you back."

---

Naturally, we hired the Lackshmi Shipbuilding Company to build the ark and made swimming lessons to anyone that wanted to them available through Lackshmi Athletics and Training, at twice the cost given the emergency situation. Humor is good medicine. Humor is a great outlet to keep us from internalizing pain. Humor allows us to see the other side. Humor allows gratitude into the heart, where there is none. Sometimes we just take ourselves a bit too seriously and need to take it down a few notches.

The board the following day:

---

### In Goat News:

"Two extremely pious goats have stolen the ark. They reason is that they would like to see a more goat friendly world, especially in India, where they don't have to worry about being run over by a family of 4 on a scooter just because the driver had to answer his cell phone to take a call from his internet provider. The last word of the goats as they sailed away in the ark was 'Enjoy the swim humans!!!'"

### Weather Forecast in Rio De Janero, Brazil

85 degrees with a chance of nudity.

---

It is a well-known fact that most goats in India are pious. The goats that are not pious are supporting a burgeoning scapegoat industry worldwide, as it seems everyone is in need of a scapegoat these days, walking around blaming everyone for everything and not taking an ounce of responsibility for our own actions. At least that is my goat theory. Most of the goats that I have seen here spend their time hanging out at Hindu temples. There are at least 10 Hindu temples that are regularly passed on bike rides around town and they all have goats. My first inclination was that they artificially inflated the attendance at Pujas, but that didn't make much sense. So until it is explained to me differently, they are pious. They are also hilarious. They are like dogs, except they eat everything and produce milk. They all have this look on their face of complete indifference and they are daring you to say something. "So what if I have been standing on this brick wall at this Hindu temple for the past 5 hours staring off into space. It is what I do. Don't judge."

The rain continued to pound, but the mood lifted. The board the next day:

---

**In Goat News:**

"The two goats accused of stealing the ark have been arrested off the coast of Thailand and returned to India where they will face prosecution for grand theft ark. Political leaders of the pious goats are lining up to distance themselves from these two goats, saying that they are extremists in piety. Their translation of the "Baaaaaa-Bleat", the holy scripture of the goats, is extreme and prejudiced. The media has labeled them as Jihad goats and their defense team is calling them scape goats. Officials at the Lackshmi Shipbuilding Corporation are running for cover as the government investigates how 2 goats managed to steal a 5,000 ton, 600 meter ark from a shipyard."

**Weather Forecast in New York City**

50 degrees with a 90% chance of apathy.

---

This happened to be Sunday, and after five weeks of rain, it looked like it was coming to an end. It would be the first dry Puja in some time. On the way to the Puja the teacher pulled me aside. I had been sick with the flu, fevers and diarrhea on and off for the past three weeks. I was sleep deprived from being in a cold, damp environment, my bed and bedding were wet and I was barely able to practice.

"Are you feeling better?" She asked me as I was just getting ready to ride the bike up to the bakery for breakfast.

"I am. I went out yesterday and bought a new pillow. It was nice to sleep on a pillow that wasn't covered in mold and dampness. It made such a difference that I actually slept through the night for the first time in three weeks." I was very grateful for the simple things, like a dry pillow.

"Good to hear. And thank you. Your creativity with the whiteboard and the funny stories has lifted everyone's spirit during the rain, and it has made a beautiful difference in our lives here. It is a testament to your character that you did this daily for the past two weeks feeling the way that you did." She went back inside. My heart smiled.

The sweat and indignity were pooled around the Yoga mat mocking me. It was 105 degrees in the room and the humidity was so high that I was sure that no modern testing equipment could measure its potency. We were 20 minutes into a one-hour hot yoga class and I was fairly certain that death was a few lung burning gasps away. The teacher was happily barking out orders and the 20 women in the class were moving in a fluid orchestration, slinging the weights around effortlessly to the rhythm of her voice. This Yoga class had weights. I knew nothing about Yoga but what little I knew did not include weights nor did it include 105 degrees.

About two months prior I had finally kicked the smoking habit, utilizing acupuncture to trick my mind into thinking I was still smoking. If I was to be free of addiction, I needed to be free of all addiction. In a larger sense, I wanted to exercise and play sports again, because they made me feel good and were enjoyable, and this was not copacetic with smoking. My female companion at the time suggested that we take a Yoga class together as a jumping off point back into exercise. This small suggestion turned out to be a major tipping point in my life and reinforced the lesson that everyone we meet in our lifetime is there to teach us something and to positively contribute to our lives, even if our perception of what has happened in real time is negative.

The universe conspires and ensures that everything in life is a learning opportunity, and when we adopt and then develop this perception of the universe we significantly progress as spiritual beings. She was standing above me, moving through the sequence, barely sweating. I didn't hate her for this but there was a definite strong dislike as my male pride was significantly damaged. The class mercifully ended about 40 minutes after I had collapsed to the mat. There were doubts as to whether Yoga, at least this definition of Yoga in a steaming hot room slinging weights around in Yoga poses, was for me. The teacher, who was a perky hyper flexible blonde in her twenties, came up to me after the class. "How was class for you?" It was an interesting question considering she saw me lying there on the floor for the last 40 minutes. So I told her. "This was yoga? Why weights? I was expecting something different."

She laughed. "This probably wasn't a good first class for you. The sculpt classes are good once you've gotten used to the practice and the heat. I would recommend coming back for a Hatha class."

I came back for Hatha, and hated it just a little less than the class with weights. But at this point in my sobriety I had started to believe in something bigger than myself. And that something was telling me to stick with this, even though it amplified every physical, emotional and pain and discomfort sensory apparatus in my being. This something inside told me that this was the good kind of discomfort that led to growth, and I had now begun to listen to that voice inside. It had helped save my life, and that belief was beginning to turn into an unshakable faith. The Yogi in me was born.

# Chapter 20

Lying in bed one morning something occurred to me that was said the first week that we were here at the ashram. It hadn't resonated at the time, but day by day was having a much deeper meaning. We were told that living in the ashram environment for six months under their rules was a microcosm of Yama and Niyama, the first two limbs of the eight limbs of Yoga which are translated as Morals and Ethics, respectively.

Ashram life differs from place to place, some being strict to the point where you cannot leave the premises for the duration of the stay and there is no contact with the outside world. This means no phone or internet, and can also mean strict diet, dress code, long periods of silence and many other disciplines designed to focus the mind. This is one extreme. The other extreme is where the student is free to come and go as they please, eat in or out and is only required to be present during class times. This is the extreme side on leniency and generally doesn't teach Yama and Niyama as part of the lifestyle of the ashram, because there is a lack of discipline.

Our experience is somewhere in the middle. We are required to be in the ashram from 6:00 pm until dawn, and that is more for our safety than a controlling purpose. It is not to say that where we are is unsafe; it is just for extra precaution, particularly at night and moreso for the safety of the women. We are expected to keep celibacy for the six month period that we are here. And that means complete celibacy, including masturbation. We are expected to be present and on time for all ashram functions and classes, even if we are sick. If we are sick for a class, we are to bring our mat and rest during the practice but it is important that we are present to share our energy.

We keep Mauna, which is silence, at multiple points during each day. These instances of silence include 10 minutes before each practice and the entire evening after the 4:30 Mantra practice, which is 5 days per week.

We must dress Indian style and dress up each Sunday for the Puja. Indian style for men is a Kurta top and comfortable pajama like bottoms and for women the same. Dress style for women is a Sari and for men the same pants with a longer Kurta with long sleeves. We must participate in all Karma Yoga duties without question including serving each other during meals. Before each class, we must stand with hands at heart center in Namaskar when the teacher enters the room. This is a sign of respect for the Yoga lineage, for us and for the teacher.

It is important to understand that nothing is done to facilitate the growth of anyone's ego, or to control behavior. There is a lesson is each of the rules. There is no alcohol or smoking and the diet is strict vegetarian. Our meals are prepared for us based on a diet that has been developed to fit the practices and the seasonality of the food over the course of the forty plus years that this Paramparya has been teaching this program. There is little to no dairy in the diet other than some yoga cultures in some vegetables and milk in the chai. And the greatest discipline we practice here is the schedule.

Yama and Niyama have five principles each and are spiritual in that they are intended to help us grow from within, and to evolve from our animal behaviors to human behaviors. They are challenging because very few of us like the personal leveling and humility provided by honest self-analysis. Our ego certainly doesn't appreciate it. The teachings of the Yamas and Niyamas stem from the Yoga Sutras, a short series of 196 sentences that codify the practice of Yoga.

The Sutras were written by Patanjali an estimated 2,500 years ago, somewhere in India. Patanjali did not create Yoga as its history trajectories thousands of years before the Sutras were written, but he codified them into a concise written format. The Sutras are written in Sanskrit, which is the oldest known language, and this language doesn't translate well into English. This is due to the richness of the language. The words sometimes require a paragraph of English translation to properly capture the essence of what was written.

Yoga is defined as the calming of the fluctuations of the mind caused by our misperceptions of the universe through our senses and then further twisted by our ignorance, ego, likes, dislikes and survival instinct. In order for us to see reality, we need to go beyond all those things that cause us misperception. Yoga has also been defined as a way to consciously evolve, as we are trying to move from our animal nature to our human nature.

The Yamas are restraints of our animal nature. They are **Ahimsa**, which is translated as non-violence, **Satya**, which is translated as truth, **Asteya**, which is non-stealing, Bramacharaya, which is the control of the creative energy, and finally **Aparigrahah**, non-greed. To fully understands the Yamas, we need to look far deeper than the literal translation and understand that there are gross levels of the Yama and more subtle levels of the Yama, and that each Yama works three ways: our thoughts and actions toward others, how we allow others to think and act towards us and our thoughts and actions towards ourselves.

People often think that they are practicing **Asteya**, which is non-stealing, because they do not participate in bank robbery or gas station heists. And while this is true and is a gross level of a Yama, we should ask ourselves how often we steal other people's time by being late or answering a phone in the middle of a conversation, which are more subtle aspects of **Asteya**.

When we practice the Yamas, we are controlling the emotional and animal part of our brain within our higher self, or the neo-cortex of the brain, and in doing so, we move from reacting to the world into responding to the world. It is a giant step to take but only about six inches of movement inside our skull from the back of it to the part just behind our forehead to be operating in the different parts of the brain!

The Niyamas are behaviors that advance our humanness. They are: *Sauca*, cleanliness, *Samtosha*, contentment, *Tapas*, discipline, *Swadiyaya*, self-examination and *Isvara Pranidana*, devotion to the higher self.

At the ashram, we were forced to practice the Yamas daily by our living conditions; the Niyamas are built into our practice schedule. The Pranayama techniques, as well as the Asana, are to cleanse and purify the body, mind and emotions. We must accept the living conditions of the ashram and find gratitude in the experience, which is our contentment. Gratitude is always a path to *Samtosha*, or contentment.

The daily repetition of the practice for six months is a major exercise in discipline, as well as a devotion to our higher self because of the spiritual growth that takes place, whether we are aware of it or not. And everything about the practice of Yoga requires *Swadiyaya*, or analysis of the self. We must hold the mirror up to ourselves and look into it.

The first two months at the ashram break us down, physically, mentally and emotionally, and then we look in the mirror and see which of these pieces we wish to keep and we pick them up over the next two months, and then the pieces along with the new growth are put together in the final two months.

Yama and Niyama are generally taught in a vacuum at first, meaning one Yama or Niyama at a time so that the student can understand the concept.  But in working form, they are completely integrated.  It is not possible to practice one Yama or one Niyama in a vacuum just as it is not possible to separate the cardio-vascular system out of a human and still call it a human being.

This beautiful foundation of Yoga is the key to freedom. Through Yama and Niyama we find happiness.  We find completeness.  Our mind is freed from irrational fear, and we become complete and healthy human beings.  We often hear people say that spirituality is for the weak, and that is the opposite of **Satya**, or the truth.  Any human willing to hold up the mirror and look at self for the purpose of advancing their growth and evolution has immense strength and integrity.  This means to step outside of the poor social conditioning that permeates our society, and into a reality based in virtue driven by our greatest good.

My knuckles were purple and almost bleeding from punching the steering wheel. Tears streamed down my face as traffic rolled slowly along through the afternoon rush hour. I was waiting to get on the ramp to head north to my apartment at a highway intersection. Always a mess this time of day. I hoped nobody could see the anger and frustration that had turned to tears.

This was the third day in a row where I had broken down crying in my car for no reason. My sensitivity to the world was on DEFCON 5 and I had no idea how to control the emotional roller coaster that ensued. Instead of driving home, I drove to the club where AA meetings were held around the clock. There was a 5:30pm meeting I needed to attend and a man to whom I needed to speak. I had heard him speak back when I first came to meetings at this club eight years ago during my first go around and thought he was all folly, and now I was going to ask him to help me. Humility comes in many flavors.

"Let's talk about the first step." My new sponsor Clive was 78 years old, and I had asked him to help me because I had witnessed over the years how kind he was and how he continually offered to help new people in the program. He was about six feet tall, and very grandfatherly. Sensible glasses, wispy gray hair that was parted to the side. He always wore a well-ironed dress shirt with no tie, a white t-shirt and tan khakis. His face was a little reddened from age, not drinking, and he had gentle blue eyes and a matching smile. He had been sober for 30 years. He was from Alabama originally and still carried with him a light southern drawl.

He was also at peace with himself, a peace that I dearly needed in my life if I was to remain sober and retain my sanity. This is what we seek in a sponsor, someone who has behavior patterns or virtues that we want to emulate, so that they can teach us through the program not only how to stay sober but how to become a better, happier person. Sobriety in AA is not so much about not drinking, because we realize at some point in time that our drinking is a symptom of the underlying problems. Our drinking was the solution, and when that solution stops working, we are considered alcoholic, so we require another solution.

That solution is the program of AA and the steps, a spiritual solution. Many people, through ignorance, come to believe that AA is a cult or a religion, and it is neither. There is the absolute minimum of organization in AA. Simply put, it is a group of people helping one another to grow spiritually with a set blueprint of recovery written very clearly in a book.

Naturally, human beings complicate it to a point where nobody really knows what is going on except a very small percentage of people with long-term, content sobriety. If an alcoholic is serious about getting sober, they seek out one of these people and ask them for help. They ask them to be their sponsor, who is simply someone that guides them through the book teaching them how to take the actions, or steps as they are called, outlined in the book for sobriety, but more importantly a way of life that no longer requires drinking.

It is that simple, and that is why I asked Clive to sponsor me. I had enough evidence from listening to him speak at hundreds of meetings and had developed enough humility to actually ask.

"I already did the first step. In fact, I have worked the steps before." While this was true, this was not the attitude I intended to take with him but my defense mechanism was on high because of the raw nerves. He had already asked me if I would go to any length to stay sober and I had said yes. Listening to him and doing exactly what he said was one of those lengths. "I'm sorry Clive, I am not feeling right. I have little to no control over my emotions right now."

He chuckled as he looked past me for a moment outside of the small meeting room we were using. This wasn't the first time he saw this. "What you are going through is perfectly normal for us in AA. We get sober, work the steps the first time, if at all, and only are able to do the best job that we can with them at the time. Think about the frame of reference. We come in here, sick in the mind, body and spirit from years of pollution and then are asked to pick up a kit of spiritual tools and use them. The fact that any of us use them long enough to stay sober is a miracle, so be grateful you have been sober three years.

Over time, as the mind, body and spirit heal, we remember more, our mind becomes healed and clearer and a lot of us end up with emotional rock bottoms without even picking up a drink. It is beautiful that you recognized this and sought additional help because a lot of people drink over it. So it is time to do the steps again, from the beginning. You asked me to start new, remember?"

This was true. I felt that I had half-assed the steps the first time through, using my counselor as a sponsor and self-sponsoring. I had managed to stay sober and was putting my life back together so that was a step in the right direction.

"Step One. Admitted we were powerless over alcohol and that our lives had become unmanageable." I read this off the wall on the poster behind Clive.

"What does that mean to you?" Clive did very little speaking and had amazing listening skills. This is how we would work together. He would ask me my thought process, I would provide it and then he would lead me to other conclusions if he thought my answers lacked mental clarity or understanding of how the program worked. We would then go to the pertinent chapter of the book if further clarification was required. Under normal circumstances, we would be in the book chapter to chapter but I was being given special treatment given he knew I had read the book 20 times and had a grasp of it.

Given that alcoholism is very much a disease of perception, it is important that perception be changed. In fact, it is imperative, because if the perception cannot change, the alcoholic eventually dies.

"It means I am alcoholic and that I cannot (or could not) manage my life anymore." This was my simple reply, and to me it was the truth. I put the caveat "could not" in there because my life was improving. I was employed and at least on the periphery doing OK. I was an emotional wreck, though, and could see how this was going to soon make life unmanageable again.

"You are half correct. The first step does not say that we are alcoholic. This is a very common misperception that people have. The first part of the step says that we are powerless over alcohol, and people do not want to admit that they are powerless over anything. Would you say that you are powerless over alcohol, and if so, do you know what that means?" He was leading me again. I really enjoyed his teaching style because it provoked me to think for myself rather than just feeding me the information. It provoked me to educe the answers from within, which is how we should learn. Educe is the first part of the word education.

"I am definitely powerless over alcohol. I would say that powerless means that it ruined my life." I was taking a guess because I actually had no idea.

"You are confusing the second part of the step with the first part. The part that ruined your life is the unmanageability caused by your obsession and addiction. Powerless means two things to the alcoholic, and this is very important to understand, especially when we get to step two and we have to admit we are insane." He chuckled with this statement.

"You see," he continued, "there are two things that every alcoholic wants to understand. Why can't I control the amount I drink once I start drinking, and why can't I quit on my own? We usually kill ourselves before we get any kind of clarity on these questions, and it is hard to seek or want clarity in a mind filled with booze, resentment, anger, guilt and shame. This is why denial is such a factor with us. We are so filled with these fears emotionally that we would rather ignore or deny an obvious drinking problem than admit all the pain we feel emotionally."

"I remember thinking that I wished that someone would explain to me what the hell was wrong with me, hopefully before I died." I added. I had thought this many times during my last 550-day bender.

"Exactly. And most of us die before we find out. We cannot control our drinking because we are genetically inclined to be alcoholic. Our bodies and minds react differently to alcohol than normal society. Normal only means how it is for most people. And for 9 in 10 people, alcohol acts as a downer, a depressant. It gives them a nice relaxed feeling. For alcoholics, it acts as an upper. Normal people want to relax after a drink or two but we want to go out on the town!

The body also removes alcohol from the system of a normal drinker at the rate of about one drink an hour, so if they only drink one drink per hour, they cannot get drunk. In the alcoholic's body, once the alcohol is broken down to a point, it becomes acetone and in our bodies we cannot break this down at the same speed because we lack either the proper amount or type of enzyme needed to do so. Acetone causes craving for more alcohol.

So the more we drink, the more we crave and so on. It explains why when we drink; we can barely ever stop at one." It was explained in black and white in the Doctor's Opinion in the book, which I had read 100 times, but reading it and understanding it within the proper context are quite a bit different.

That is the purpose of a sponsor, to provide context for the directions in the book and to act as a guide. This hit me hard but it was so plain to me. When I had first done the steps 3 years prior, I had simply admitted that I was an alcoholic, despite the fact that I had no idea what it really meant, in the context of recovery. It had lifted such a huge weight off my shoulders just losing the denial that I had figured the step was done correctly. I looked back at my drinking and tried as hard as I could to remember a time when I went out and had just one or two drinks. I could not, no matter how hard or long I thought about it! Now that I could clearly see the problem, and what the problem really was, it explained to me why I drank like I drank and also how what I thought was normal was actually abnormal. It was a freeing moment, and I also understood very clearly why I could never safely drink again. My mind may want it, but the body can't have it.

"And unmanageability?" He peered over his glasses as he asked me the second part.

"I am clear on that. Multiple arrests, multiple hospitalizations and the embarrassing behavior, not to mention the terror perpetrated on the nervous system and the emotions, the physical body and the mind." This part was crystal clear to me and had been for some time. In group therapy we had put together a list of what alcohol had done for us versus what alcohol had done to us as part of testing unmanageability, and that exercise made it quite obvious.

We parted ways for the evening and the drive home from the club was much more pleasant than the drive from the bus stop. I felt peace for the first time in some time.

Chapter 22

My birthday happened to coincide with the day that I was elected president of the students at the ashram! It wasn't actually President, it was a new Karma Yoga role called monitor, where the person is the liaison between the teacher and the other students and acts as a monitor for student behavior for the rules that we were to follow during our stay.

The monitor also assigned labor for projects that were completed on Mondays which was group Karma Yoga day. Naturally, I renamed the role "President" and put out a press clipping on the whiteboard that I had won the Presidency in a dirty campaign funded by the Lackshmi Corporation.

Like any good politician, upon election I broke a campaign promise and immediately implemented a new tax. At the ashram we were expected to keep Mauna, which is silence, for certain periods of time. Mauna does not just mean silence, it means to avoid communication, verbal and non-verbal, with others unless absolutely necessary, which is a loophole because absolutely necessary has a different meaning from one person to the next. Mauna was a practice that allows us to look within, rather than always communicating outward.

Mauna allows us to practice patience, and not immediately verbally react to the world, simply because we are eliminating the outgoing communication channel. It forces us to think before we don't speak! It teaches us that not everything that we say is necessary, or in my experience, most of what I say is not actually necessary.

It is a *Tapas*, or discipline. It works on our ability to respond, rather than to react. But most importantly, it teaches us to listen. It is a good practice, that when practiced enough, becomes very pleasant, because it changes our perception of the world. It is also incredibly difficult, if not impossible, for people that lack self-awareness. We were to specifically practice Mauna every day 10 minutes before each practice, and from after the Mantra class to the following morning after Hatha. We had no Mauna on Thursday and Sunday. In reality, outside of sleeping time, we practiced Mauna a total of about 90 minutes a day where we weren't in our rooms. It was a disaster for half of the students.

I decided that as President I would monitor Mauna violations and each violation would be a ten-rupee tax. This translates to about $0.12 cents. In addition, I told everyone that I had a mole helping me monitor, because the behavior of people was to only keep quiet when the teacher was around, rather than actually making an effort to practice Mauna. I had reached the unintended objective of most politicians and was immediately hated by the constituency.

The results of the two-week taxation period ended up being a beautiful sociological study and a microcosm of society. Six students were involved; 3 women, 3 men. Two of the four women had 15 and 14 violations, one woman 8 violations, two of the men 3 each and one of the men zero. When the results were shared with the group the following feedback was collected. Names of the students are not being used to protect the innocent until proven guilty!!

- Student #1 with 15 violations claimed they were above the law.
- Student #2 with 14 violations claimed ignorance of the law.
- Student #3 with 8 violations agreed with the spirit of the law but felt that it was being unfairly applied to them.

- Students #4 and #5 had 3 violations each and agreed with the law.
- Student #6 had zero infractions and was a zealot of the law.

In our little microcosm society, 17% of society thinks that they are above the law, 17% claim ignorance of the law, 16% agree with the law but think it is unfairly applied to them (the victim part of society) and 50% agree with the law and obey it. Nobody was willing to pay the tax!

# Chapter 23

Two days after the step one meeting with Clive and the completion of step one I was at work in downtown Seattle and my phone was ringing. It was Clive asking if I was going to be at the meeting and available to start step two after the meeting. Absolutely, I assured him. Still riding high from the positive emotions and self-knowledge gained from our last chat I looked forward to the discussion.

The stars were just coming out as I pulled into the club parking lot. Rush hour had made me late for the regular meeting by ten minutes. After parking the truck, I filed into the room and took a seat. In the 8 years I had been coming here on and off, this room hadn't changed a bit and at the 5:30 meeting, nobody with long term sobriety had changed either. This was reassuring that people could actually stay sober, even through difficult times. The meeting topic was Step Two. Towards the end of the meeting, I jumped in to share.

"My name is Gary, and I am an alcoholic. I am grateful, that by the grace of God, I am alive and sober today." This was something that was always said. It was a reminder for me and a reminder for anyone who cared to listen that this is a spiritual program, and given the number of times that I should be dead, it is only by the grace of whatever God there is that I am still breathing in this body.

"I want to simply share how I came to believe in a power greater than myself, because I know that a lot of people struggle with the concept. We come in here with many religious misconceptions that are wrapped in emotionalism. These emotions prevent us from being able to see the truth. Please let all this go when coming to step two, and find something to believe in; or if you cannot find something to believe in, our book says that willingness to believe is the only requirement to move forward with the spiritual solution. When I came in my higher power was Karma, or universal law. The simple law of cause and effect. It was easy for me to believe in because I had been on the wrong end of it for so long! Thank you for letting me share." I could see Clive smile across the room. A major reason I asked him to help me this time around was because he was a very spiritual man in his actions and words. He had a beautiful awareness and kindness in his soul that radiated wherever he was. I was looking for this in myself and hoped he could teach me the actions to take to get there.

After the meeting there was some small talk and we retired to the smaller room across the hall. Over the past three years my concept of a higher power had grown considerably from Karma to basically divine universal power. I used the term God simply as a way to say the same thing but I didn't believe in God by any religious definition. Religion and I had parted ways at age 14 and there was no going back. Religion was unnecessary to me, as I believed that God resided in every human being and that when we seek within, the divine is there.

From that foundation, we begin to see the divine in every being, in everything, and we build a beautiful bridge that is a connection to the universe. I often referred to this as God's grace, this feeling of ultimate tranquility. I felt it from time to time in moments of high gratitude and thankfulness for simply being alive. Being just thankful for being alive is a beautiful act of humility. Clive knew this and was not concerned with the first part of step two. Step two read: "Came to believe that a power greater than ourselves could restore us to sanity." He was more concerned with the sanity portion of the step, so much so that he asked for a complete sanity test.

"The big book simply refers to insanity as picking up the first drink over and over again knowing that we can't stop. That is the only insanity in reference here. People get really hung up on this and think that it is all the crazy things that they do when drinking." He chuckled at himself here probably remembering some of the stunts he had pulled under the influence. "The crazy stuff we do when drinking is caused by a mind filled with booze, which lowers the inhibitions. You don't need to be alcoholic to do crazy things on a mind filled with booze." He was correct there. Society was filled with this on every weekend in every city in America.

I jumped in "Clive, I understand this step very clearly, particularly in light of the revelation of step one last night. I am still shocked at how long (not really long at all) I have been around the program and am just now understanding step one. It is like my mind didn't want to hear it."

"Yes, I know you do." He smiled, and I knew there was more to it. "I would like to suggest that we look at other areas of your life for other addictions. This is normally something that we do in Steps 6 and 7 but we are going to do it here. We have an opportunity to live addiction free and often times we just transfer addictions from alcohol to another substance or lifestyle. Do you like shopping?"

I looked at him with as puzzled a face as I could muster without laughing. It wasn't possible. Starting to openly crack up, I replied. "I have a thing for women's shoes. I wear them only on Friday night, only salsa dancing. It is very difficult to find women's shoes in a men's size 13, but I do my best."

Clive didn't know whether to laugh or not. He had heard almost everything in his years of sponsoring people, but after a moment of seeing me with a huge grin, he laughed. "OK, that was the easy one. Drugs? Gambling? Gossip? Working out? Workaholic?

Sex? TV? Smoking? Food? Think about what you spend your time on and where your mind is at."

This was a great question. If we wanted to live a happy life, it would have to be addiction free, of everything. Replacing the addiction with another would not fix the underlying cause. I thought through his list. Drugs weren't my thing. I didn't enjoy gambling as much as I enjoyed drinking at casinos. Gossip made me ill. I had recently started and was enjoying yoga practice and found it to be spiritually expansive but hadn't ventured into any other physical activity yet. I worked a fair amount but it wasn't excessive. No dating so sex was not an issue. I watched sports on TV only, and had quit smoking a year prior. Food was not an issue although I had a sweet tooth that needed monitoring.

"This is a good exercise, but in reviewing your list there is nothing that I would consider addictive. My thing was extreme alcoholism." As I said this my mind was still wandering through a typical day for me, looking for anything that was extreme.

"OK well then let's move on to step three, which says 'Made a decision to turn our will and our lives over to the care of God, as we understood Him.' While there is not a lot of action in this step, it is obviously a big decision. What are your thoughts on this?" He went silent, and would give me time to gather my thoughts. I had practiced this step for some time to mixed results. I was interested in hearing his take on my mixed results.

"I have been doing the third step prayer since I got sober. The results seem mixed." I wanted to say more but there were no more words.

"Did you make the decision before doing the prayer?" Again he was very clear about the step and what was required for it to work in our lives.

"I think so. To be honest, when I first got sober, I just wanted to stop drinking so I am not sure what was going on. This step is supposed to shrink our ego, I know that, and to put God in control of our thinking, but it seems that I still do an awful lot of thinking on my own." This was my current understanding. Clive was very kind and patient and could see where I had holes in my practice of this step.

"Part of the beauty of this program is its simplicity. To grow in spirit takes courage, but it is not difficult. We make it difficult as humans because we love to complicate things for our ego's sake. It gives us a nice feeling of self-importance. The third step says to make a decision to turn our will and our lives. This doesn't mean we stop using our brain. And we are only making the decision here; no further action is required beyond the decision. The action is the next 9 steps. You are correct that there is humility associated with this step because we are subjugating our ego. We take this step because the alcoholic is an example of self will run riot. And I think that you would agree that your willpower got you into the mess you got yourself into. This step gives us a new boss, a new director for our lives. Are you ready to make that decision? And keep in mind, God wants all of you, not just the bad parts that you want to release." He smiled again that beautiful, gentle smile that reassured me that this was all going to work out very well. There was happiness and contentment at the end of this journey as he was sitting there in front of me.

"Yes." I said simply.

"Good." He replied. "Let's say the third step prayer together."

"God, I offer myself to thee, to build with me and do with me as thou will. Relieve me of the bondage of self that I may better do thy will. Take away my difficulties, that victory over them may bear witness to those I would help of thy power, thy love and thy way of life. May I do thy will always. Amen."

# Chapter 24

The alarm on the cell phone started braying at 4:45 am, rousing me from a short sleep. The usual surprise of opening my eyes to a dark open air room in India hit me and the immediate thought was how many mosquitos and other insects were sharing the bed space with me, even with the mosquito net in place. I stumbled out of bed in the morning darkness knowing full well that we would not see the sun for another 90 minutes. It didn't matter the morning, there was always confusion and slow thinking, even though the body had felt progressively better as the time marched forward here in our six- month Sadhana.

I followed the usual routine and ate a couple of light cookies, or biscuits as they were called here, had some water and got dressed for Hatha. I grabbed some camphor, two incense sticks and a lighter and headed down to the main practice room. The beauty and perfection of the pre-dawn silence was only broken by the light tapping of a knife blade brushing a cutting board in the kitchen from the morning tea preparation. Hope was making the tea this month and it was always nice to see her beautiful smile first thing in the morning. I had become very light on the feet and my footfalls were silent as I moved into the main practice room to prepare for the Arthi.

Like all good things, my presidency came to an end, which simply means a new month started and we were awarded new Karma Yoga duties. This month was I given the role of teacher's assistant. This role included ringing the wake up bell and the bells before each practice, which was a total of eleven bells per regular day. In addition, the practice area was set up for the teacher, including a small floral arrangement in a clay pot, incense and the teacher's mat.

It also included preparing for the morning and evening Arthi, including all the supplies, which were camphor to light the flame and incense. It was the most time-consuming of all the Karma Yoga duties and required the most discipline.

I was happy to be a simple bell boy, out of the limelight of the fake presidency, the fake daily press conferences and the pressures of holding a fake high office. It was a humbling experience. Karma Yoga was an exercise in *Tapas*, the third of the Niyamas, and it is usually translated as discipline. The practice of discipline is relative to the individual. People without drinking problems do not need to exercise discipline with the amount of alcohol they take. I do. The practice of *Tapas* though, like all of the Yamas and Niyamas, is to embody discipline as a part of life; to make it second nature.

As I stood in the foyer just after ringing the 5:00 am wake up bell, I pondered the *Tapas* in my life. Since I had gotten sober, *Tapas* was always present in the maintenance of my spiritual condition, a necessity of quality sobriety. I believe that when we have to maintain our spiritual condition, and expand our spiritual condition as a way of life in order to survive, it becomes our second nature whether we want it to or not.

I was noticing this overlap in Yoga and AA more and more as I progressed here at the ashram, and I noticed more and more how AA had ingrained in me the Yamas and Niyamas, just using a different taxonomy to describe what I was doing. It was a beautiful comparison. I had an obvious flaw in my *Tapas* and that was a sweet tooth, and it was a constant struggle. Sometimes I just gave up and convinced myself that I would have to work on it in my next lifetime, and other times I gave up sweets completely for a few months at a time. There was no middle road on this one. I looked at my watch and saw 5:20 am, time to ring the ten-minute bell for morning Arthi and get on with another day of Sadhana.

# Chapter 25

The immediate effects of turning my will and my life over to the care of the divine would not become readily apparent to me. It is something that occurs over time by having awareness of the decision, but I had a sense of ease inside me that wasn't there before for just having made the decision on such a conscious level. Being aware of the divine working for me in my life and understanding that everything that happens was for a divine reason would eventually turn to faith. I realized this now. It was always right in front of me to see, but I couldn't see it through the emotionalism. The book says that this decision is the foundation that our life is to be built on moving forward. I could feel this foundation forming in my heart, a strength and ease that was never there before budding like a lotus in the dawn light. It felt right; it felt like a light entering the dark tunnel of my soul, a feeling that was new to me.

Step four of the AA program stated that we 'Made a searching and fearless moral inventory of ourselves.' I had done this before in the first year of sobriety by following the instructions in the book, which were very straightforward. But as Clive had stated, once the mind has cleared from the fog of addiction and active use, there are many things that are not addressed in our first fourth step, and we have to revisit them. That is one of the beauties of the program. It is forgiving; we don't have to do it perfectly, because it is a kit of spiritual tools that we can always return to when needed.

We met at a coffee shop near the club. Coffee shops are a favorite hangout of people in recovery because they don't serve booze and they do serve caffeine. It is a safe place to socialize. Clive looked tired today. He had recently taken a job, at age 79, for some extra income. He liked the role but it was a lot for him at his age and sometimes it showed. He had darkness under the eyes which were more visible through the lens of his glasses.

"Did you bring a sheet of paper and pen?" he asked, glancing around the shop. There were at least four regulars from the club here and probably more that he knew, being an old-timer. There were the usual throng of people pretending to be very self-absorbed and busy, their eyes bugging at the importance of what was on their computer screen and headphones plugged into their brains shutting out the reality surrounding them. Off in the corner a few women were gossiping about their office and whether or not someone named Claire was going to get fired for being late for the umpteenth time. Two of them were in favor of the firing, acting overly appalled at her consistent tardiness. Three sets of couples were sitting at the window just passing the time people watching. It was apparent that two of the couples were in a good space; they looked happy. The other couple was doing everything in their power to frown and not acknowledge that they were together. Clive's question pulled me from my daze.

"I brought two pens!" holding up a notebook and a couple of cheap Bic pens.

"Good. Before we get to that, how are you doing? Did you have a nice week?" He was always kind enough to want to understand how I was. He sought to understand the people around him and I always cherished this and worked to add this to my list of personality traits.

"It was a nice week. I spent a lot of time reflecting on the decision to turn my life over. While it is completing unnerving on the one hand, there is a lot of comfort in it. Like a weight of worry has been lifted. So long as I don't focus on the outcomes it feels good."

This was the extent of what I could say at this point in my growth but I had apparently hit upon a key point.

Clive's smile widened. "It is nice that you mentioned outcomes. In this program we say one day at a time. And we say that in early sobriety because it is necessary to stay sober. Even one hour or one minute at a time depending on the severity of the individual. But as we spiritually grow and gain time in sobriety, the meaning of one day at time changes to a plan for living. That is what this program is, a plan for living. It seems like AA is a society for not drinking but that is just poor perception. In this plan for living, one day at a time means to stay in the moment, to live in the moment. This can cause some level of confusion because people have insurance policies and have to plan, of course. But I think that it means to stay in the moment emotionally. This is a key component to sobriety because it is our emotions being all fouled up that got us in here in the first place, and to an extent, what brought you to me, three years into your sobriety."

I let that sink in. What a beautiful point. His wisdom was potent. "So what can I do with this sheet of paper?"

"Write the word 'Resentments' in the top left corner and list all your resentments, top to bottom, leaving a space between each one. Keep it simple and short – economy of words. Then in the second column write 'Cause' and put the cause of the resentment top to bottom. Then in column three put 'Affects my'. Here you want to put what part of self is affected. There are three choices: sex, self-esteem or security." I wrote the columns in my neat, block lettering across the top of the page. This was straight out of the book. He continued. "Column four is where we get tripped up. Ignoring what the other person did, write down our part. And in column five, write down the root underlying cause. That can be selfishness, ego, carelessness, whatever it may be."

I didn't remember the last two columns from the book. My first attempt at this had only the first three columns and it was obvious to me that I had a part in everything but it was left at that. We have a lot of sayings in the program and one is "More will be revealed." There was a lot of truth in that simple statement, especially when paying attention. I didn't say anything but Clive could tell from my reaction that this part was new to me. "We list in column two how society has come in conflict with us. In other words, what *they* did. It is impossible to come in conflict with society without society at least being partially to blame.

When we are in addiction, we blame society. And the further we get from the event, the more society is to blame and the less we have any part in it. That is how the disease changes our perspective. But, if that is true, then it almost must be true that we are at least partially to blame." He was looking directly at me to see if I had absorbed the point. I had. The realization hit me like a wrecking ball smashing through a building. The wall I had built up around my perfectionism came crumbling down and I realized in that moment that I was responsible for everything that happened in my life. It was staggering. It only remained to be seen *how* responsible I was.

"I am responsible." I said this aloud but so weakly it was really to myself. I must have had the dumbest look on my face. Clive could see the realization spreading over me.

"There is nowhere left to hide after we do step four. We see the truth about ourselves, about our behaviors. The only decision left from here is what to do about it. It's like the new person that comes to AA arguing about whether or not they are alcoholic, or a person going to a doctor and finding out they have hemorrhoids. Your opinion of it doesn't really matter. What are you going to do about it? That is what matters. When you complete the resentments section, complete a section on fears, then on guilt and shame and finally on sex. So four sections. I am sorry to be short this week but I have a church group meeting to attend." With that he smiled and stood up to leave.

I spent the next several hours into the evening working on this, and over the next few days adding to the list on my sheets of paper. There were 93 items when I was satisfied that they were complete. In 92 of the items I was at fault, or had done something that set into motion the chain of events that led to me being resentful, fearful, guilty feeling or sexually upset. It was a brutal, yet refreshing reality. All of the negative emotions that I had been suffering from for years were of my own doing, and what was worse, I had been blaming others and letting them control my behaviors for all that time.

I decided right then and there that not only was I responsible, but I was empowered to not let others control my emotions. The sense of freedom was overwhelming and I thanked God for this opportunity to have this deep self-awareness. It occurred to me that whether a person is alcoholic or not, this is a wonderful lesson for anyone to learn. We turn on the news, or just look out the window and see the hatred, the anger and the ignorance of society, driven by fear and insecurity, and it is all self-induced suffering. It made me feel blessed to be an alcoholic, because most of society will never have the opportunity to take this step, and will remain in the suffering.

I looked at the first name on the list, my ex-fiancée Karly. The pain that I must have caused her was unbearable to think about. How could I have been so selfish? How could I have been so emotionally unavailable? My self-righteous attitude was so overpowering and my ego so out of control that I used her weaknesses and fears against her to crush her soul. To crush the beautiful love that we had. And she kept trying to love me. She saw *something* in me and continued to put up with me, not understanding how or why I had changed. I didn't understand.

I can imagine her lying in bed alone at night, me down on the couch passed out in front of the television, crying herself to sleep asking what went wrong. Or worse yet, blaming herself for the drastic and nightmarish changes that had occurred in me, seemingly overnight and out of nowhere. The verbal abuse, the ignorance, the projection of my self-hatred on her. How she must have been thinking why she wasted 10 years of her life with me. I could see it now. How could I not? It was written in black and white in front of me, by my hand, my penmanship.

There was nowhere left to hide; I had to own this. And it hurt more than anything I had ever felt before. The anger, the ego, the self-righteousness all became crushed under the weight of this new reality and a sense of humility entered my heart. Through the stark pain shattering my emotional core, a sense of courage and humility was finding its way into my being. For the first time in my life I realized that ownership of our wrongs meant freedom from them, and I swore to God and all that is divine that from this moment on I was responsible for my life, my thoughts, my words and my actions, even if I wasn't completely sure how to do it.

I then moved onto the fifth column. After a careful review I did a count. 54 instances of being selfish, emotionally selfish to be exact but selfish all the same, and 38 incidences of being self-righteous and egotistical. It showed me very clearly the person I had become.

Not the person I was, but the person I had become through my behavior and twisted perception that it was the world's fault. It made me sick, and I didn't want to be that person for another second. And the root cause of all this behavior was a list of irrational fears, based deep within the ego. Fears that were based on threats, real or perceived, to my basic instincts of life. But something happened that was completely unexpected. I looked at the paper and realized in stark clarity how these fears, resentments, guilt and shame had been controlling my life for more years than I could count. I also realized that control over life came from how much time we spend in thinking patterns.

What is our life if it is not our thinking and from that wellspring our actions? That is our real life, not the amount of wealth we accumulate, the job we have, the number of degrees we have. What we think defines who we are, and when I could see on paper, in black and white, written by my own hand, I could see that I had become my fears, resentments and guilt. I shuddered with the realization and felt incredibly dumb for allowing this to happen.

It seemed to have happened without my conscious knowledge. But another realization occurred to me. What was on the paper was so ridiculous looking and so irrational in nature that most of it immediately melted away and a beautiful feeling of relief washed over my soul. I immediately wanted to share it with someone, and it just so happened that I would get the opportunity to share it with my sponsor as part of step five.

## Chapter 26

"We all take a shower from time to time, correct?" The Guru flashed his warm smile around the circle of us students in the evening **Satsangha**. I was sitting on the floor with a small pillow lifting my pelvis a mere inch off the floor. This allowed me to sit with my knees to the floor and the spine perfectly straight. It had taken over three months of severe discomfort and change to the body to get there, but I could now sit on the floor. This was considered a major win for the course and my Asana practice and if I was incapable of doing nothing else, the asana practice was considered a success. The Guru continued, the flickering of the candle in the wind making the light dance in front of him.

"We are discussing **Sauca**, the first Niyama, and it means to cleanse or be clean. It is so important that Patanjali devotes two Sutras to it. Most people believe that if they take a shower on a fairly regular basis that they are practicing **Sauca**, and they are missing the boat. **Sauca** is probably better translated as "purity." We must cleanse and purify the body, inside and out, the emotions and the nervous system, and the mind in order to properly practice **Sauca**. In this ashram we practiced Shanka Prankshala, the cleansing of the digestive system, a practice of **Sauca**.

We then practiced the eleven day Pranayama technique, a cleansing of the nervous system and mind. Our diet at the ashram allows the internal body to stay clean, maximizing our efforts here. We must remember that our mind has a memory slot for everything that we have ever seen. Every commercial, every movie, every act of violence, every internet site, every book and every person. Our nervous system carries all these memories as well. So to become

101

cleansed, it all must go, and that was the focus of the first two months.  Many of you had deep physical manifestations of the cleansing including diarrhea, sweating, itching, and sleeplessness. These things are all normal as we purge the body of these impurities. We must then focus on how to live a lifestyle that does not refill the impurity tank, and that is a conscious choice that needs to be made by a conscious mind."  The Guru stopped and fiddled with his long grey beard, pausing as if he had a new revelation.  He picked up the cup of tea in front of him and sipped it slowly, allowing his last comments to sink in.  Looking around and seeing that everyone was still awake and at rapt attention, he continued the discussion.

"Patanjali says that when we perfectly embody **Sauca**, we become indifferent to our body and develop a dispassion towards others.  We lose all of our hang-ups, or better stated judgments of self.  And when we lose judgment of self, we lose judgment of others. I find it ironic that the *vast majority* of Western Yoga teaches people to have hang ups with their body.  It is not Yoga because it is teaching the opposite of Yoga.  Moving towards the height of purity is moving towards an undistorted universe, and we cannot do that if we are worried about the length of our hamstrings and whether or not our Tree Pose will look good in a photograph.  When we become pure, we are ready to see ourselves, and the universe will show us."

# Chapter 27

Clive was surprised to hear that I was excited at the prospect of sharing my fourth step with him. Most people in AA dreaded the step, not only because it was felt that we had to share all the skeletons in our closet, but because a good sponsor corrected the sponsee's fourth step as a teacher red pens a student essay, and we felt judged. A good sponsor will offer perspective based on not only their own experience, but the experience of the people that they had previously sponsored. It was a glorious spring day so we met outside at a small table in front of the club. There were two tables and at the other table two people sat chain smoking, looking like they were newer to the sobriety game. Their eyes darted nervously about, seeming worried that someone might see them in a known place of sobriety.

They were rather shabbily dressed and both had gloves with the fingers cut out. The male was wearing a beat up leather jacket, torn jeans and hadn't shaved in weeks. His hair was beyond unkempt and one of his front teeth was missing. The woman had on jeans two sizes two small and had her back to us. She had a tattoo across her lower back. It said something but her body had become misshapen from lifestyle and it was illegible. The folds of her sides hung over the jeans from a shirt that was too short. She had a baseball cap on with her hair stuffed up under it. Clive looked over his shoulder at them and then back at me.

"We must not judge. Everyone deserves help if they seek it. Maybe if they attend the meeting later you can ask if he needs a sponsor." He had been suggesting that I find someone to sponsor for about 3 weeks now and I had yet to act on it. But with that thought, we got to work.

I shared my entire fourth step with Clive. He had very few comments and seemed pleased at my effort. Most often in a fifth step, the sponsor will correct some items in the columns regarding what part of self was affected and have discussion on whether any of the items belonged on the list in the first place. More than anything a sponsor provides clarity. This is true of any spiritual guide; their primary role is to provide clarity that allows us to remove ignorance. Learning is educed, rather than induced. This process of sharing our deepest and darkest secrets with another human being is cleansing and very similar to the Christian process of confession. I started calling doing a fifth step with a sponsor confession without the guilt. When I was raised Christian I was taught "sin as often as you like, so long as you come to confession all is good." The fallacy was that once a certain point of sinning is reached, confession becomes out of the question and the Church has built in a lifetime of guilt for not only actions, but thoughts. This was the teaching of my Catholic upbringing.

I now realize the fallacy in that as a teaching. We never learn anything about ourselves except to repeat the same behavior or to feel guilty. There is no improvement built into the process. Spirituality teaches that answers come from within and that divinity is everywhere and that we are free to believe in that divinity as we see fit. Spirituality teaches morals and ethics that are self-monitored. Not only did I feel like I was walking on air with my head held high with a sense of purity, I had learned about the gross character defects that were governing the types of behaviors that caused me all this trouble in the first place. And once we understand our character defects, we can now work on eliminating them, or at the very least minimizing them in our life. And this work happened to be just around the corner with steps six and seven, which we started in earnest.

104

Step six states that we are ready to have God, as we understand Him, remove all of the defects of character. Defects of character are the items listed in column five of the fourth step, and we make a decision from our heart that we are ready to change. It is a small exercise but a big step, because this is where we decide the action that will change the person we were, with those character defects, into a new person without them. And sometimes that change can be frightening, because we are not sure what we will look like on the other side of that change. We also have a tendency to become attached to our character defects and use them as a crutch. We don't want to let them go because these defects and our ego allow us to blame the world for our problems so to let them go means there is nowhere left to hide. So this decision moves us further along the path of living as a responsible human being. I had no desire to let go of my self-righteous attitude, because it made me feel good to be right all the time, or at least my perception that I was right all the time. But once it was let go, I realized that the ignorance created by self-righteousness was preventing me from learning, preventing me from growing and preventing me from behaving as a responsible human being.

And then step seven is simply asking our Divine to remove these character defects so that we don't repeat our mistakes. There was more to it than that though. Clive looked up from his Big Book after reading this section together and started in on the practical application of the steps, the action items.

"As usual with this program, we ask God, but we must take the action. Our higher power gives us the power to take the action. Your primary character defects seem to be an overweening ego coupled with low self-esteem or self-worth (these two go hand in hand), and extreme selfishness. We can't just pray this away. We have to act, because faith without works is dead, as our book clearly states. What we do to remove character defects is that we behave, or take actions that allow us to behave, in exactly the opposite manner. Our behavior then changes our thought pattern, which then changes our belief system. The new behavior essentially becomes habit or second nature. You may or may not notice that this is the reverse of modern psychiatry. In that field, people are given information or self-knowledge and awareness eventually changes the behavior. That doesn't work with alcoholics. First off, most of us don't have time to gain this sort of self-knowledge given that we are half dead from heavy drinking before we make it to a meeting ready to listen. But more importantly, self-knowledge does not provide us the power for recovery, because we are powerless. We need the power from something greater than ourselves to give us the strength to take the action." He finished there to see if this was going to sink in. It was incredibly profound, but made logical sense. If I don't want to behave a certain way, behave in the opposite fashion until it becomes our primary nature. Not much to it!

"I see it. It is quite profound. So what do you suggest?" I had no idea what the actions were that I needed to take but I was all in on this program. It was having an amazing and positive effect on my life and happiness was growing in my heart each passing day.

"Try to perform acts of selflessness, no matter how small. Open doors for people. Smile at strangers. Do things for people without *any* expectation of *anything* in return. Only a selfish person will do something for someone and then expect a reward. Stop thinking of yourself so often, good or bad. Force yourself to think of others. In your morning meditation, pray for 5 others minimum, especially your enemies or people you may not like. Pray for everyone on your fourth step resentments list, for their well-being and happiness. Do it every day. Keep close to your gratitude list for humility. Recognize that we are all the same, that you are no better than or no worse than *any* other human on this planet. Shut your mouth every once in a while and listen. Not just to others, but listen to self. Try not responding or even practicing some periods of silence. You will eventually realize that nobody gives a damn for your opinion. In fact, if you like take a sheet of paper and write down in order of importance the top five people whose opinion of you matters most. And then work on that sheet of paper until it is blank. This will free you from fear of acceptance, which is tied into all your character defects. As we love and understand the self, we become our natural self and no longer have to act to garner the acceptance of others or worry about what people think of us. The program itself is a constant reminder of humility. We come in here dragging our wounded asses, half dead, divorced or on the way to being divorced, facing criminal charges and on and on, and then take step one and big spoonful of humility. Each step provides an additional sense of humility. Stay connected with all the steps. This program is a way of life. A way to live our lives happily and sober." He finished with his beautiful smile and closed his book, signaling we were wrapping up for the day.

"I never thought happy and sober could exist in the same space, Clive. I am incredibly grateful for your wisdom and your help." I had hurriedly written down all his suggestions in my notebook. It was quite a list of action items for what seemed like such small steps. But I was excited to start down this path. I did not like the person I had become, and while the first five steps had made a profound change in who I was, I could see that steps six and seven were where the rubber met the road.

# Chapter 28

We were told early on in our ashram stay that we should make spiritual friends and not develop attachments to people as it would affect our Sadhana. I became good friends with one of the students almost immediately. I decided that I probably wasn't going to make Moksha in this lifetime anyway so some personal attachment to people would be OK. We shared the same twisted sense of humor and had similar business backgrounds; basically our view of the world and how it worked were quite similar. His name was Rahan and he was from Northern India. Retired now three years at the age of 40, he had owned a company that supplied rickshaw parts to the gazillion motorized rickshaws that are seen everywhere in India.

They are the Indian taxi cab, and are designed as a three-wheeled motorcycle, one in the front, two in the back. The driver compartment is small and narrow, open air and the most prominent feature is always the horn. In India, the horn is a source of great pride and used frequently, for every driving occasion. Cow in the way? Honk the horn. Goats crossing near a temple? There is a horn for that. Pedestrians walking down the shoulder with no chance of even coming close to them? Use your horn. Bicyclist taking up the lane? Use your horn *and* go over the center line into oncoming traffic to pass.

And while in America these taxis would have a limit of three passengers in India that limit was often stretched to eight. I was convinced that all vehicles in India are designed as clown cars for the circus because there are always an unimaginable number of people climbing out of a vehicle on any given day. The same is true for scooters as we have witnessed a family of four tooling down the road on a scooter, small child in between the driver's legs, mom holding a baby side saddle with the driver chatting away on the cell phone in rush hour traffic. And don't ask about helmet laws.

Rahan and I were discussing this on one of our frequent visits to the coffee shop. We actually had many conversations like this that bordered from the sublime to the serious and from the absurdly hilarious to the philosophical. We were the brainchildren of the Lackshmi conglomerate when we were assigned to cleaning the bathrooms together.

We frequented many coffee shops and stands in India ranging from corner stands where your bike is parked and you walk up and have a quick coffee to the newer European style cafes that are starting to pop up. The standard coffee in India is served in a small cup and contains about one ounce of coffee, three ounces of hot milk and ten teaspoons of sugar. Rahan was always informing me that if the spoon wasn't standing straight up in the sugar then you weren't drinking a true Indian coffee.

Today we were sitting at one of the more European shops, owned by a woman in her late 50's from Belgium. She had short thick, grey hair and glasses that had the rim flat on the top and rounded on the bottom. She always smiled and asked us how our Yoga was coming along when we visited and was very kind to us. Her café was on a secondary street in a small, lazy town near the ashram. Mostly foreigners were found to be lounging about at the outdoor tables in this café, as the town was an experiment for an international community started about 50 years ago. The original founders of the town had raised considerable capital from multiple governments to fund the town and it was said that almost every nationality in the world could be found there. The experiment was to have a town with no currency where people would use just what they need and come to the town and provide different services in exchange (without barter) for what others needed. So for example, if one was a dentist they would provide dental work for the town free of charge and if the dentist needed vegetables for dinner, they would simply go pick up vegetables from the vegetable farmer.

This utopia worked for some time until the humanness of people surfaced and the combination of greed and sloth and the founders of the town who governed it passed away. Too many people moved to the town and became freeloaders and did not contribute to the society but expected to receive all the other goods and services free of charge. This, coupled with lack of effective leadership after the death of the founders, effectively killed the original idea. It reminded me of almost every other place in the world where people purposely try to freeload off the government and either use excuses and blame for their inability to contribute to society or were simply just too lazy to contribute.

Rahan was about 40, had shaved his head for the stay at the ashram, and had a goatee and mustache. We had the same thin, muscular build and were about the same height at just over six feet. I had remarked to him that in America once a guy shaves their head that there is a law that states unequivocally that a goatee and mustache must be grown. Otherwise, there was no sense of style to the look. I also mentioned to him early after meeting him that he could pass for a New Yorker, given his fairly light skin for someone from India. He became highly offended by this and didn't speak to me for a week.

He was playing with the handlebars he was trying to grow on his mustache as we launched into one of our stream of consciousness discussions. As I looked out onto the street noticing cows and goats walking by the thought of driving in India popped into my head.

"It is very odd to me that there are so few accidents on the roadways with the utter chaos of people, animals, farm animals and vehicles coupled with the complete lack of attention to traffic laws, or even what Westerners would call common sense," I said as the waitress brought me a latte. In this café the coffee was more Western style and a nice latte cost just over a dollar.

He spoke both Hindi and English and had a clean accent with a good grasp of English, even though he tried to sell himself off as not having a primary language. Since he retired three years ago he has been travelling the world so he had a perspective that most people don't have. Wisdom is defined as knowledge plus experience. I see a lot of people in the world, especially in America, with knowledge from university, but almost no experience. Americans don't travel much per capita internationally, and when we do, we tend to stay in commercialized places that closely resemble America. It gives us a very narrow view of the world and no sense of detachment and discernment from our view of how the world actually works. Rahan had wisdom.

"People here have a much higher level of awareness on the roadways than we do in the West. They have to; otherwise traffic casualties would be the leading cause of death in India. What about the guy the other day on the scooter with six adult goats strapped to it – all of them pious I might add. That guy was probably headed to a Puja. Indian drivers develop an awareness of the traffic fluctuations as a sixth sense, which is why there are so few accidents." He was cracking up but this was commonplace in India. To him it was normal but he had travelled enough to know that it wasn't the norm in other countries. He was ordering a second coffee as I pondered this.

"I would think Westerners should be very careful on Indian roadways because we are conditioned by so many traffic laws that we are completely unaware when we drive. I find that to be interesting commentary and an analogic microcosm of society at large, because America is largely under the illusion of its own senses, unawareness is the norm. People are asleep at the wheel of life in America." I grinned at the analogy eying a glass case full of cakes,

111

brownies and other goodies. He stopped grinning for a minute with a smile that would charm a snake from his basket. This meant we were moving into a more serious arena of conversation.

"India is being ruined, or already has been ruined, by the infiltration of the American way. The destruction of cultural virtue that has been a part of India for thousands of years is under full assault, and it is done so simply and innocently that hardly anyone notices it in real time. It begins with advertising and a flood of goods to the market. The constant barrage of advertising, or to consume for the sake of consumption, drives what people think is need. It plays to the ego. A country that used to have the virtue of **Samtosha** (contentment), built into its society, comes under attack. People begin to desire what they see advertised, and when they don't have the resources available to buy those things that they perceive everyone else has, there is frustration.

Only people don't really know why they are frustrated. That frustration boils over into all sorts of societal problems, as India is witnessing. Higher crime and violence, further class separation between rich and poor..." He fell silent for a bit after this, scratching at the bottom of his goatee, his mind considering other points. I agreed. I didn't need to be handicapped with a degree in sociology or psychology to see this, the lost art of common sense and critical thinking were all that was needed.

We both fell silent for a moment in our thoughts, what he said didn't warrant much of a response from me because I agreed with the sentiment. He began browsing through the newspaper while I checked my email. He suddenly threw the folded newspaper down under my nose.

"See this? This is what I am talking about!" I glanced down and was looking at a half page ad that provided online Pujas. A Puja is a Hindu ceremony usually held at a temple, much like a mass. It is a celebration of the divine. He was flummoxed as he continued.

"So now people can sit and watch Puja on their computer at home, hopefully with their own pious goat, and don't even have to get out of bed." He rolled his eyes and sat back in the chair with his arms folded. I chuckled a bit and saw the similarity to the West.

"Rahan, this isn't a surprise to me. We have this in the West, I am sure. But look at the bigger picture. In the West there are thousands of companies that don't want you to do anything but look at their content, twenty four hours a day, seven days a week, so that they can generate the highest advertising dollar. Think about it, Facebook would prefer that society was on Facebook all day, every day, and got all their news and all their needs met on Facebook, by looking at a computer screen, tablet screen or mobile screen – and Facebook is not just in the West. Our cable companies want the same, as is the app war going on. All the advertising pollutes our mind and nervous system and dehumanizes us, but we are addicted to it as social conditioning. The best thing I did was get rid of cable, put ad block on all my search engines, tablets and phones and stopped listening to the radio. I don't watch the news because it is all bullshit designed so that you watch their content. MSN has gotten so bad at wanting clicks that every story on their site requires a minimum of 10 clicks to ready the story. It is ridiculous what these companies are doing in the name of greed. So it seems the content battle is beginning in India as well." I had worked in the technology industry in financial leadership roles for over twenty years and understood the game and what companies did to drive their value, real and perceived. At the boardroom and executive level, it was all about the money, all the time, and nothing else. I had never participated in an executive meeting that wasn't about the bottom line, and every decision was based on profit margin, directly or indirectly. Rahan knew this from his experience, even in India. He sighed.

"I don't think the world can handle 1.5 billion Indians at the per capita consumption level of the United States. Between India and China, either we will destroy the earth or it will destroy us, and I am betting on the earth destroying us. We, the humans, are an endangered species, yet in our arrogance we continue to march on this path of mass consumption for the sake of the accumulation of wealth." His phone started to ring with the end of this thought and he took the call.

# Chapter 29

The plane touched down in Buffalo, NY at 12:10 am in January. Dry, light snow blew sideways across the runway. The rough landing said that the wind was coming in hard off Lake Erie. I visited my hometown of Buffalo, NY in January for one reason, and that was my mother's birthday. It was just after Christmas at the beginning of January and also saved me from traveling over Christmas and New Year's when airfare was three times the cost and the airports were three times as busy. But it was cold. This trip was special for me because I was going to complete the amends process with my parents for the harms that I had caused them during my drinking.

The purpose of the amends process in AA is to make things right for the alcoholic in the physical world. We are physical, mental and spiritual beings, and the AA program works on those three levels, with the first three steps getting us right with our spiritual selves, the next four steps with our mental selves, and steps eight and nine with the physical world, which includes getting right with other human beings that we had harmed. Step eight asks us to make a list of all persons we had harmed and to become willing to make amends to them all and step nine is the amends process. It states "Made direct amends to such people wherever possible, except when to do so would injure them or others."

As usual with the steps, context and education from Clive was required. He said that it was imperative to understand that making amends is not running around to apologize to everyone. Making an amend is not making an apology, although it can include one. It is about making things right with the other person without mention of anything that they may or may not have done. This last point is important because the purpose is not to create more issues by pointing out faults in the other party. The conversation generally starts with explaining that we are recovering from alcoholism and as part of the healing process we have to make our relationships right in the world, and most importantly, that we are asking the person to help in our recovery.

If they aren't too mad at us, there is usually some understanding and at least a willingness to listen. We then make our amends, which may include an apology for wrongs to the person. If we owe them money, we figure out a way to pay it back. We are again careful not to mention anything that the other party did as we are just trying to clean up our side of the street. Once we have finished talking we give the other party the opportunity to say anything that they want. And we listen, without argument, without commentary and without a voiced opinion. This last part can be painful. He also noted that I had already completed step eight, because my list was on the step four sheets. I just had to become willing to make the amends.

In reviewing my step four worksheet, I really wanted to make amends to Karly, my ex-fiancée. However, in conferring with Clive, he recommended that this not take place. She was remarried and happy, had ceased contact with me years earlier and to reinsert myself into her life would cause unnecessary harm. As much as it hurt me because I felt a sense of needing to cleanse my guilt, he was right. We cannot make amends to someone if the process of doing so would harm them. It was suggested that I pray for her well-being and happiness, from the deepest place in my heart as amends to her. The second name on my list was my parents, and this trip was a nice opportunity. My brother would be there too, which was good. He was also on the list. Amends can be tricky because there is often an expectation that when amends are made that the person accept us back into their life. Fear of acceptance by other human beings was one of the main fears that drove the way I lived my life for so many years and this had loomed like a dark cloud following me through the entire recovery process.

I would try to see over the cloud, around the cloud and through the cloud and it just felt darker and more oppressive. However, as I continued to trust the process of recovery, there would be intermittent holes in that dark cloud and the sunshine that was surely on the other side would glisten through for a few moments, and from that, hope would spring. With each amend, the cloud got smaller, the fear of acceptance withered on the vine. What if people didn't accept me now that I didn't drink? What if people didn't like the "new me"? What if I had become boorish and was viewed as a teetotaler? All seemed legitimate fears.

Again, the program showed me its merit when I trusted the process and took the action. Some people on the list could not remember or did not perceive what I had done as a wrong. Some people on the list were so happy that I was finally getting the help that was so desperately and obviously needed to everyone but me that they welcomed me entirely. I had one person who said that they didn't really like me much when I was a drunk and didn't really care for me much now! But slowly but surely, I felt that I could begin to look the world in the eye again, the guilt and embarrassment of my behaviors being rinsed and rung out of me like the rain built up in the raincloud that was following me on this path, disappearing into a sunshine and happiness that I never knew existed.

My brother picked me up at the arrivals area. It was bitter cold and the thermometer read minus 5 degrees Fahrenheit. At that temperature, everything feels desolate. Cars appear to move slower, everyone that is out on the street is indistinguishable from the next due to layers of coats, boots, gloves and scarves. And even though I had grown up in this city, I could not understand how people still lived here. The winters were long and harsh, with brutal stretches of vein chilling cold and crunchy piled snow that never seemed to melt. We

117

made the 15-minute drive to a northern suburb of the city as if moving through a ghost town.

The following day we were relaxing in the living room and I decided to begin the amends process. For them, my major wrongs were being unavailable. When I thought back on how I had behaved the last two years of drinking, I think there were times when I went four months without even a phone call. And while they didn't say anything to this issue of being unavailable per se, the awareness was there to know that this was devastating to them. And the few times there was communication, I was such a drunken mess that the conversation was pointless. As the thought process of the conversation entered my mind, I remembered back to one time in particular.

I was out of money and out of alcohol, with the exception of a 90-year-old bottle of whiskey that had been given to me by a neighbor before I moved to Seattle. I vowed that it would never be drunk. This is folly with any alcoholic, because eventually every drop of alcohol in the house will be consumed unless there is some intervention of help, either by the self or others. I had just drunk the entire bottle and was beyond drunk, even for me. It was during a time that my cell phone was actually working and I called them to tell them that I just drank the most fantastic whiskey, the words slurring from my mouth. I hadn't realized that it was the first communication between us in three months. It was an incredibly embarrassing moment in a string of embarrassing moments.

But for them, the important thing was who I was now, and what I was doing to stay on the path of recovery. My parents' virtue, which I had never recognized either in their teaching it to me or during the 25 years of my drinking, was so obvious now. They were not complex people. Married 44 years at this point, they had had me at the age of 18 just after high school. They struggled the first few years of my life and then when things were a little more stable my brother was born.  They instilled in me the virtues of hard work and earning, honesty, courage, perseverance, support and had sent us to Catholic school to educate us theologically, but once we were of a certain age, we were free to choose our religion, if we desired one. This is not to say they were perfect or the upbringing was perfect, none are.  To take two people who have stayed together for 44 years and raised three children with those life lessons is an amazing accomplishment in this day and age.  I felt constant guilt about ignoring most of the teaching, but also saw that now in recovery it came easy for me to follow these virtues, which were the same principles of the AA program.

It wasn't a struggle for me because the software was installed in me as a child and I was now incredibly grateful for this.  There are so many people in the program who are not as lucky to come from a stable and love filled home.  Often people in AA come in from broken families, families in addiction, no families at all, foster families, wards of the state, juvenile centers and then they are in a position to learn virtue in the program for the first time in their lives.  And while the reward for them is great, they don't have the benefit of the social conditioning that I was so blessed with by having a family that cared for me, even if I was in ignorance of their teaching.  The Hindu belief system is that our souls choose our parents and the family that we have when we enter our body at birth. When I learned this viewpoint and pondered it, it made sense to me why I chose these beautiful people to be my parents.  Whatever karma there was to burn from my past lives, I wanted to be born into a family that would teach virtue as a basis, independent of the obstacles that needed to be overcome to live them.

I simply told them my story.  The entire story.  And what was important about this conversation more so than any conversation that I had ever had with my family was that I was emotionally engaged and sharing with them not just the highlights of my life like it was being reported in a newspaper, which was my usual communication method, but I shared what I was thinking and how I was feeling. I communicated to them with connection, which as far as I could remember, I had never done.

This communication had a profound effect on explaining who I had become as a person as a practicing alcoholic and as someone now three years into recovery. I learned that amends don't need to always be apologetic, but sometimes just being caring and present enough to allow people to know that you are there. One of my father's favorite expressions growing up was "lights are on but nobody is home" and it pained me to think that most of my life I had been communicating to them in this manner. The realization that came from this simple, yet long, conversation changed the entire dynamic in our family. We developed a unity that had been missing for 43 years. It was one of the most beautiful and compelling moments in my life, and it opened a window to them that I had never seen. I felt like for the first time in my life they really knew who I was, and conversely, this beautiful window allowed my mind's eye to open so wide that I now saw the reality of who they were.

At the end of step nine the program says that there are a set of promises that come true for the alcoholic in recovery. Given that steps 10 through 12 are maintenance steps and meant to continually enlarge the spiritual program these promises are appropriately placed at the end of step nine in the AA text. They read as follows:

"If we are painstaking about this phase of our development, we will be amazed before we are half way through. We are going to know a new freedom and a new happiness. We will not regret the past nor wish to shut the door on it. We will comprehend the word serenity and we will know peace. No matter how far down the scale we have gone, we will see how our experience can benefit others. That feeling of uselessness and self-pity will disappear. We will lose interest in selfish things and gain interest in our fellows. Self-seeking will slip away. Our whole attitude and outlook upon life will change.

Fear of people and of economic insecurity will leave us. We will intuitively know how to handle situations which used to baffle us. We will suddenly realize that God is doing for us what we could not do for ourselves. Are these extravagant promises? We think not. They are being fulfilled among us—sometimes quickly, sometimes slowly. They will always materialize if we work for them."

I read these carefully, and had probably read them 500 plus times in various meetings. The words were meaningless until the steps were completed. They were like a fairy tale told to child to guide their morals and behavior or words from a child's game. Step on a crack, break your mother's back! As I sat on the plane from the connecting flight in Chicago back to Seattle these words felt like a part of me. They were no longer just words read at a meeting, words on a piece of paper; they had come to life, and had manifested in my heart and very being. For the first time that I could remember the slate was clean, and from this clean slate, a new life could be formed, a life free from the constant fear of the future, guilt from the past and disease in the present. That sense of grace that was becoming more commonplace in my heart welled up inside me as the plane began its ascent, and I dozed off, with the love of God and all that is good about the universe encompassing my being.

# Part Three

## Let the Will of the Universe Be Done...

# Chapter 30

Rahan and I were just getting ready to leave the coffee shop when Moji showed up. The other male student at the ashram was on foot, wearing a tacky red derby hat, short ponytail sticking out of the back, and sported a pointy black goatee. He had walked the three kilometers to the coffee shop. The rest of the students had purchased bikes to ride around to eliminate the need for the crowded buses and to provide some efficiency in travel but Moji rarely left the ashram, so he opted to not get a bike. Rahan and I were shocked to see him, so we decided to stay for another coffee.

"You guys leaving just when I get here?" Moji said this with more than a hint of sarcasm, which was a new character trait for him. Or it was a new character trait that he was just now showing to us after almost four months of living under the same roof. Seeing that we were now staying, he placed his 5'-8" frame into the chair opposite me. He had on thin framed glasses and hadn't shaved in a while, the gristle starting to blend with his long, dark sideburns.

"We were so shocked to see you outside of the ashram that it required another cup of coffee." Rahan interjected with the same level of sarcasm.

"No doubt, you have changed profoundly since you first arrived." I added with no sarcasm. He was smiling, and that was a new thing for him as well.

"Come on! I am the same now as the day I showed up." He was dead serious when he said this. I looked at Rahan and started laughing my ass off, and Rahan was so shocked that he couldn't express an emotion one way or the other. It was like insane humor and shocking disbelief were fighting for the use of his brain at the same time causing an emotional gridlock, so he just sat there looking puzzled.

"Moji, you come on. When you got here the first thing you asked me was why I was so happy. And I had replied that I was happy for a lot of reasons. Remember what you said? You said two things: One was that you asked me why I was in this program if I was already happy, and then secondly you said that you were still looking for happiness, which is why you were here. At least one of the reasons anyway." The memory of this brief conversation, which occurred on about the third day we had met, jarred his memory and his attention immediately focused. From my desire to help others, this was called a teaching moment and I hoped that I could help him.

"Yeah, and it still doesn't make sense to me why someone happy would come here." He said that but was pondering something else. To not lose him, I jumped back in.

"Remember my response? Happiness is but one step in spirituality. We just learned that we actually have to transcend all emotions, including happiness, on the yogic path. But it is tough to move anywhere on the spiritual path in misery." Saying this got his attention back so I continued.

"I have seen this in AA so many times. We are always the last ones to see our spiritual growth, and then people point it out to us, and we again hold up the mirror and finally start to see it. The first two months you were incredibly impatient. You yelled at almost everyone in the program, including the teachers. You almost got in a fight with an old lady on the bus!" I had been giving him grief about that incident for months now, at least now he could laugh about it.

"She deserved it," Moji said this with a sly smile. Our coffee showed up and Rahan began his usual Indian ritual of putting sugar in his coffee until it turned into paste. Indian coffee is served five parts milk, one part strong coffee and between 10 and 20 parts sugar, depending on the individual. Rahan was still dumbstruck. Seeing that he wasn't going to add anything at this point I continued.

"So you are stating that you were happy when you arrived. OK. Ponder this at your leisure. Everything that we project in speech and action is a projection of self. The universe is a reflection of us, meaning that what we perceive is a mirror of self. Our senses go out and attract what is going on inside us. You attract conflict because you have conflict inside you, and then you project that conflict back out. We must remove the part of self that is projecting conflict. Or to put it another way, it is the law of attraction at work."

He was shaking his head.

"I don't agree with that." He said this, but he didn't believe himself, and I think he was confused by my hypothesis. I took another approach.

"Moji, you say you haven't changed. OK. You agree that you got into arguments all the time during the first two months here, right?" I was going to lead him down the path with questions.

"Yes, but they started it each time. I actually have a list in my room of people that owe me apologies and what they did." He was dead- serious about this and got upset when I spit my coffee all over the table laughing.

"Are you kidding me?" My look of complete disbelief must have shocked him. "We should really discuss that but let's not get off track. In the last two months you haven't had one conflict with another human being at the ashram and in fact have been smiling, pleasant and fun. How do you account for that change?" He pondered for a moment and replied in the same manner but with different words.

"I haven't changed; it is all you that have changed. Since you have all changed, I haven't had to add anyone to my list." He was scratching his goatee as he said this. I knew we were close to getting to the realization. Very close. I had seen this in AA many times, including with myself. We set out to get sober, finally quit drinking and working the program. The program slowly changes us, but it is not so profound a paradigm shift all at once that it is noticeable, at least for the vast majority.

There are people here and there who have white flashes which they term spiritual experiences and the change is obvious but most are of the educational variety and happen slowly over time, imperceptible to the person making the change until hindsight becomes available to them well after the fact.

In Yoga this is called **Swadiyaya**, or self-examination, and it is the same. We have to learn to examine ourselves in real time, and it is a skill that is developed through practice. In the close living quarters of the ashram, we have people constantly holding the mirror up to us. I was now holding the mirror up to Moji. I continued with the discussion turned lesson.

"It is true that all of us had changed in the past four months, it is not possible that we haven't. It is also not possible that you haven't. As for your list of people that owe you an apology, throw it out, life is too short. And remember for every apology that you think you are owed on that list, you owe one back."

# Chapter 31

"I am going to jail." Marcus looked at me with an excitement on his face that I didn't expect with this statement. He working on Step 3 and had asked me a couple months ago to sponsor him. Marcus was about 6'-4" tall with short cropped brown hair, much like a military style cut and a thin, muscular frame. He had been in and out of institutions his entire childhood and hooked on drugs and alcohol since age 13.

He was now 25 and going to jail for one year for felony theft to support his drug habit. It was nice that he finally realized there was a problem. He had asked me to sponsor him because he knew me when I drank. His father and I used to drink together and he was at my favorite bar every once in a while. He was amazed that I was sober and not dead. I told him I was amazed that I was sober and not dead when I shared the part of my story with him that he did not know.

"Ah so you had your court today. Sorry to hear that you are going away." I wasn't sure what to say as I had never known anyone in this predicament.

"It's OK, I deserve it. I am going to find a sponsor in jail and continue with the program." He added this taking a sip of coffee.

We were in an empty room in a downtown YMCA that would soon be filling with drunks of all shapes, nationalities, sexes, religions, races and sizes for a meeting. Alcoholism does not discriminate. It was Friday and Friday was what I now called Service Day. Now that I had completed the first 9 steps I was in the maintenance steps of ten, eleven and twelve and step twelve was about carrying the message to other alcoholics by sharing at meetings and sponsoring others. It is said that we cannot keep our sobriety unless we are willing to give freely of ourselves to others.

This is called service work in AA. In Yoga, it is called Karma Yoga. It is doing something for another human being or human beings without the expectation of anything in return. Giving of self. It provides us with humility and grace and to me is one of the most life fulfilling endeavors I have ever encountered.

In reality, I had been practicing steps 10 and 11 since the beginning of the AA program since it is suggested by every sponsor, and then we move to step 12 after we complete the first nine steps and are considered properly prepared to assist another alcoholic in their sobriety. Step 10 is an end of day review of our thoughts and actions, and if in that review we find that we have come into conflict with society, we are to make immediate amends.

This is to keep our slate clean in real time. Step 11 is completed in the morning and is often called morning meditation, where we set our intention for the day, pray for the alcoholic who is still suffering, and ask our Higher Power or the Universe to direct our thinking. In Yoga, step eleven is referred to as **Isvara Pranidana**, which is turning one's will over to the Divine. There is an entire branch of Yoga for this named Bhakti Yoga.

I relished in the practices of Step 10 and 11 because it was a beautiful practice of **Swadiyaya**, or self-analysis and it constantly taught me lessons of my behavior. But given that my primary character defects were extreme egoism and emotional selfishness, my sponsor highly suggested that I move into service work and sponsoring others.

This was a direction that I would follow in a deep and meaningful way because the tradeoff was a deep and beautiful sense of humility and gratitude that I could not reproduce under any other circumstances.  In addition to sponsoring people, I took a service position as secretary of a regular meeting on Friday evenings, secretary of another meeting on Wednesday afternoon and volunteered my services at a recovery center near my home.  I estimated that 15 hours a week was spent in service work to other alcoholics, and every minute of it was a reward that only could be explained in the heart.  This type of service work gave me tenfold what I gave to it.

# Chapter 32

Rahan and I ambled out of the coffee shop out into the dusty, noisy street. Sidestepping a pile of cow dung we went over and unlocked our bicycles for the ride back down to the ashram. Moji had left earlier as he was on foot and we all had to be back in time for the 4:30 Mantra practice with the Guru. Getting the bike turned out to be a great decision. In addition to the cardio-vascular exercise, it allowed for a lot of freedom and speeds up travel considerably. As we got on the bike I made the following remark, in the most casual manner I could. I was trying not to burst out laughing as the outcome of the comment was not in question.

"Wow. Rahan, check out that beautiful woman." His head snapped around like one of Pavlov's dogs hearing a bell. Total social conditioning combined with the survival instinct of reproduction.

"Where? Where?" He was glancing here and there lost and confused as no woman was coming up on the radar.

"Right there." I pointed over towards the immediate storefront net to the coffee shop. Exactly five feet away from us. His face went through a series of emotions in two blinks of an eye; from disappointment, to confusion, to recognition, to anger at being duped, to a sly smile.

"Come on man. That is a mannequin..." He was shaking his head as we pedaled away.

"You have to admit, a very attractive mannequin. And did you see that dress?" I added coolly.

We were in the fourth month of six months of celibacy. Complete celibacy, which means no self-pleasure. Voluntary celibacy. We discussed it often and weren't sure which was worse, the fact that we volunteered for it or the fact that we were keeping our word on it. It was expected as part of the ashram lifestyle. Rahan was single but had a taste for women during his many travels. I was in a relationship and missed my girlfriend terribly. Something had to give, and the mannequin had possibilities.

The practice of celibacy in Yoga is often referred to as **Brahmacharya**. This is somewhat of a misnomer. Bramacharaya is the 4$^{th}$ of the Yamas and it means to control creative energy, one of which is sexual. So in a sense, in can be practicing celibacy, but it is a very small aspect of the Yama. I viewed the celibacy as more **Tapas**, a discipline that we needed to keep. It was also a practice that allowed us to subjugate our survival instinct. In order for the human race to continue, we are given sexual urge. It is completely natural and a gift of the universe. However, it is part of the survival instinct and part of our animal brain, and when we practice Yama or Niyama we are subjugating the lower levels of our brain to the neo-cortex, allowing us to further evolve as human beings. Subjugating our survival instinct allows us to increase our ability to think before we act. Another practice to subjugate survival instinct is fasting.

As we pedaled back down to the ashram, our home of Yama and Niyama, we laughed at the lunacy of our practices as viewed by the outside world, but were grateful for the virtue we were adding to our life. Our studies were largely focused on why people suffer and what can be done to alleviate this suffering. Patanjali in the Yoga Sutras states that greed is the number one cause of human suffering. That desire to take and want more and to want it now. The parallel to this with people in addiction is stunning. I have met thousands of alcoholics and drug addicts in my time in AA, and every one of them suffered from the disease of want. When we look at the word we can see it so clearly.  Disease = "dis + ease" meaning that we are not at ease.  This means we don't feel good.

When we don't feel good, especially between our own two ears, we are suffering.  Pain in this life is not an option, we are going to have that, but suffering is optional as it is a function of our mind and of our own doing.  To broaden Patanjali's statement, all human suffering stems from lack of virtue.  We hear musicians say ad nauseum that "love is the answer".  This is another way of saying that virtue is the answer, only we humans get virtue all tied up in religion and create chaos out of it.  Virtue does not require religion as religion is a creation of mankind, and for the most part it has been historically created so that people can be controlled.  Virtue from spirituality requires no religion, as all answers come from knowing thy self.  Alcoholics Anonymous is a program for living that gives the alcoholic virtue, where there was little or none, eliminating or shrinking to manageability the thousands of irrational fears of the mind.  Yoga is a practice that leads to virtue and knowledge of self.  Two spiritual programs, one destination.

As we walked our bikes into the parking area at the ashram I thought to myself how amazingly grateful I was that the universe has seen fit not only to save my life, but to steer me into two remarkable spiritual programs, both entirely different on the surface, but to the spiritual man, the man who is awakened and can see the reality, see beyond his senses, likes and dislikes, ego and other distortions of perception, he sees one path.  He sees a unity of spirit.  This man looks beyond the cover of the book that says that AA is to help drunks get sober and sees that AA exists to align and bring unity to a person sick in mind, body and spirit by giving them a spiritual path of virtue and plan for living where they *don't have to drink anymore* and can use that path to grow and to evolve as an empathetic and contributing member of society.  This man looks at Yoga and doesn't see an underweight flexible twenty-something blonde woman in stretch pants posing for a photo holding one leg over her head while balancing on the other. He sees a plan for deep self-awareness and virtue designed to bring the human being above the norm, above the soul sickness of the world's lack of virtue, and into spiritual evolution and awareness.

This is the lesson. What can we see beyond our senses? What is the bigger picture? As I unlocked the door to my room to grab a quick nap before Mantra practice, I felt blessed that I was now seeing the bigger picture. And the biggest picture was so simple. Virtue is the solution to man's suffering. Only so few will do it, because it requires us to hold a mirror up and admit to ourselves, that maybe, just maybe we are wrong about something. And our ego, so bloated and out of control from years of social conditioning and poor teaching, and our mountain of ignorance, this inability to see things for what they are, prevent us from even thinking that it is possible to pick the mirror up. We want to look in the mirror but it weighs 1,000 pounds, and we are terrified at what we will see. And rightfully so.

## Chapter 33 – 3 Years Ago

Beasley Coliseum in Pullman, WA was decked out in full regalia on a bright spring day in May. It was warmer than usual for this time of year and the sun was baking through the black cap and gown I had donned for graduation from the Executive MBA program. My parents and brother had flown all the way from the East Coast and then driven with me the five hours from Seattle to Pullman to watch me walk, at age 44.

I hadn't walked either in high school or for undergraduate, with both of those graduation certificates arriving in the mail with no fanfare. As I sat in the second row of the floor seats of the basketball arena I looked up into the seats searching out my family. I was again filled with a beautiful peace and love that stemmed from a deep gratitude for the life that had suddenly been given to me.

How was it that four years ago I was near death from alcoholism and now graduating with an MBA, and a 4.0 average to boot? These moments of gratitude and humility made me realize the beauty of the universe through self-realization and the spiritual path. I felt God's grace as if I was being touched with a micro piece of the universe and all the vibration of the peace and harmony that is the universe was included with that touch.

I felt the gratitude for my parents, for whom I always had such a hard time relating, and how they waited patiently for me and accepted me for who I was for 40 plus years to become the man I was supposed to be. They never complained, and I never noticed until objectivity was reached by overcoming self. Then I could see clearly not only their beauty, but the beauty of the virtue that they instilled in me from childhood. They say in the Hindu culture that our soul chooses our parents because of the lessons that we need to learn based on our past lives Karma. If that is the case, then I clearly understood why my Atman chose these two. I don't even know how to begin to show them the gratitude that they deserve for raising me with the virtue they did, even if I did ignore it and didn't have the ability to see the truth right there in front of me. I guess that all I can do is live my life the best I can, and ensure that they are a material part of it, which is what they want anyway.

I had enrolled in the MBA program for no particular reason; it was just something that the divine drove me to 18 months ago. Ever since I had begun practicing Step 3, turning my will and my life over to the Divine and it began working for me in my life, I simply followed the direction. It felt good to have completed the program, including a two- week international study in China and what became known as the 18 month death march.

The MBA program was 18 months of 30 hour weeks, with rolling five-week classes including a Leadership class with 8,000 pages of reading. With the volume of reading in that class, it was easy to get Plato's Republic mixed up with The Confucian Dialects. The difference between the MBA and the undergraduate degree in Finance that I received from the University of Maryland was that this one felt earned. I slogged my way through undergraduate school in six and a half years, spending most of my time during these years practicing to become an alcoholic later in life rather than studying. I had little realization that I was majoring in vomiting, hangovers and memory loss from evenings blacked out.

In AA, it is said that we must always expand our spiritual base. Yoga is also a continual growth process up the spiritual path, which is non-linear. In the West, we like to think of everything as linear, and in spirituality, we learn fast that it is a series of concentric circles each one above getting smaller up to an apex. And we sometimes have to take a step or two back to move forward, relearning a lesson that we may not have learned properly the first go-around. Increasing wisdom is increasing spirituality and wisdom is gained through the combination of knowledge and experience.

Everyone has wisdom to some degree, but knowledge without experience is just repeating something memorized in a book, and experience without knowledge can be dangerous and all over the board. For example, if someone would like to experience parachuting, they should learn how to pack their chute first.

As I walked down the aisle to collect my diploma from the president of the university, it occurred to me how I used to think about how I could function without alcohol in my life, and now I think how did I ever function with alcohol in my life.

# Chapter 34

*Tapas* Tuesday rolled around again and I decided that discipline was not really needed for Mauna or fasting. When we practice *Tapas*, it should be for an area of our life where we would like to add discipline or change. If a person does not have a problem showing up for appointments on time, then that person would not practice *Tapas* on showing up for work on time.

Today I decided to tie *Tapas* Tuesday to *Swadiyaya*, or self-analysis. The entire stay at the ashram is an exercise in *Swadiyaya*, but today I wanted to narrow the focus. From my spiritual journey in AA, I had learned to become a selfless individual rather than a selfish individual, and this occurred through taking actions that were selfless that eventually changed my thinking. This change in thinking eventually became habit and that changed my behavior, or nature.

Where my habit or nature used to be to think of myself first, I now considered the other person first before acting. Of course this didn't happen all the time, it is impossible to be completely selfless, but it made a remarkable improvement in my life and how I felt about myself. My interest today was testing to see if I was still behaving selflessly. I decided to consciously perform at least five acts of kindness during the day as my *Tapas*.

In contemplating this exercise it proved to be a beautiful example of *Swadiyaya*, more so than *Tapas*. It would give me the opportunity to decide after the exercise if I needed to consciously practice more selflessness or if it had indeed been instilled as part of my nature. I went through the day with this intention, much like the practice to Step 11 in AA where in morning meditation an intention is set for the day and then most importantly, acted upon. Without action, nothing is accomplished. Then at the end of the day I reviewed my actions and thoughts of that day, seeing if I had met the intention and any other actions that I took to cause conflict with others. With this self-examination in place, it was humbling to see the change in real time.

One level of **Ahimsa**, or non-violence, is to reduce or eliminate conflict with other human beings. In fact, when we practice **Ahimsa** to the point where we begin to embody it, we stop attracting violence and conflict to us. As with all Yamas, **Ahimsa** is a three-way street. Are we practicing non-violence towards all other living beings from the gross to the subtle level? Are we ensuring that other beings are not violent towards us, in word or action? Are we practicing non-violence with ourselves, in word, thought and action?

This final piece of the triad was one where I fell down often. I had spent so much time during the stages of alcoholism in self-hatred that negative self-talk was commonplace, and something that was a constant effort to correct. I couldn't help but notice that my exercise in **Tapas**, which was really an exercise in **Swadiyaya**, had an **Ahimsa** component to it and also tied directly back to at least two of the steps in AA.

At the end of the day I reviewed my actions. I had performed at least six acts of kindness that I was consciously aware of, and in reviewing these acts of kindness, they were all actions that I would have taken subconsciously anyway, because I had performed them at the ashram outside of the scope of this exercise. Analysis at the end of the day falls under Step 10, and I also noticed that I had not come in any new conflicts with anyone.

This review of my actions helped me to understand that I had become a selfless person in thought and action and also provided a deeper understanding of how the Yamas and Niyamas are shared behaviors. Once we start to practice one, we cannot help but practice others. The one we choose to focus on becomes a gateway to the bigger picture. I am certain that this is not by mistake. It is the same with the steps in the program. While they are taught and practiced piecemeal, once the program is in action they go hand in hand with each other as we move up the spiritual ladder and grow.

"Why are you here?" It was a question that the primary teacher in the yoga teacher training was asking all of the new students, or yoga teacher aspirants, in the first session. Fifteen women, an older gentleman, and I sat in a small studio room in 95 degree heat being generated from 8 space heaters along the 20 foot high walls.

Mirrors ran along the long side of the room, approximately 30 feet long and the mirrors went from the floor to 7 feet up the wall. This was a city studio, and the design of it was very chic and hip. Black and white paint with a modern art feel, the people that practiced here were cool and elite. At least that was their portrayal of self. The pricing in this studio was set accordingly. The floor was a gray rubber with some give and sweat pooled on it rather than being absorbed. The lead teacher for this training was standing in the front of the room giving us the preliminaries of the teacher training program, which was brand new to the studio. We were to be the first graduating class.

He was about 30 years old, informed us he had been teaching Yoga for some 12 years and had studied for about 1,000 hours with different teachers worldwide. The training program of the studio was primarily designed from his experience with some assistance from the three other teachers at the studio.

"Why are you here?" He asked again. A perky woman in the front, an obvious fitness nut, said she wanted to teach hot power Vinyasa to kick-ass music. Some said they had no intention of teaching, and were there to deepen their personal practice and knowledge of yoga. Some wanted to teach part time to supplement their income or simply to supplement their soul. It is common knowledge that it is difficult, if not impossible, to make a decent living teaching yoga. Unless you are in the top 1-3% and are considered a rock star that offers teacher training to many people, teaching yoga full time usually involves agreeing to a life of meager means. Most teachers have either other income sources or their significant other is the bread winner of the family and it is a part time and enjoyable endeavor. When the question came to me, I say quietly for a moment, deciding what to say. Without having an answer, the first thing that came to my mind came from my heart.

"I have no idea." This was the absolute truth. I signed up for yoga teacher training because the little voice inside me told me to do it. That same voice that had been prodding me along from the inside since the day I was hospitalized with delirium tremens. Only now I both heard and listened to that voice. The cost of the training was considerable in both time and money, lasting six months around a full time job with a lot of hours and cost $3,000. It was physically rigorous and mentally demanding and I had only been practicing yoga for two years up to this point. There was a strong belief that this was what I needed to be doing so I signed up for it, without reason. I had no intention of teaching.

We end up asking ourselves the age-old question, why are we here? Patanjali says that we are here to experience life and to achieve Moksha, or that reuniting with the Universe. That was good enough for me; I was in teacher training to experience it!

# Chapter 36

Ten of us sat in a circle, a single candle flickering in a light wind that blew through the outdoor hut at the ashram. This space was octagon shaped and it was called the Patanjali room, representing the 8 limbs of Yoga. A Patanjali statue adorned the north wall facing south, which is also traditionally where the teacher faces. The room was about 20 feet across and a perfect octagon, with cement walls that ran up from the tiled floor to about four feet. From there dark teak wood slats crisscrossed up to the six foot base of the ceiling. Each of the sides then went further up to form the top of an eight sided pyramid at about twelve feet.

The candle threw off minimal light as the ocean breeze gently blew through the openings in the side of the small structure, and the dancing flame bounced from face to face as we prepared for the evening's activity. Rahan was sitting cross-legged, his knees resting comfortably on the floor, and he could probably sit like that for the duration of the exercise. We would be chanting Om for the next eight hours as part of a tribute to the Guru's Guru before him. This was the date of his Samadhi, or the date that he left his body. We would each chant Om and then pass the Om to the next person and continue to go in a circle until sunrise. We estimated that at about six seconds per Om that we would chant 4,000 times before sunrise. That is a lot of vibrating with the universe.

Om is considered the king of mantras, and it is also said to be the vibration of the universe. When we chant Om, we are trying to come "into tune" with the universe. When chanted properly, we can feel it starting in the lower part of the body and traveling up the spine as we extend the chant. Here at the ashram, we chant Om before and after everything we do. During the first two weeks of being here, Rahan and I estimated that we would chant Om 20,000 times per person during the normal daily schedule over the six months we were here. This did not include special events like this one! Twenty thousand Oms.

As the evening wore on in the Patanjali hut, the cooking staff at the ashram brought us fresh fruit to eat including papaya, coconut, banana and pineapple. Plenty of water was available as well as Indian coffee and Chai. Something happens when we chant, not only just Om. Chanting is a form of concentration, or Dharana, which leads to Dyana and even Samadhi.

I think we all noticed that at some point during the evening that there were blocks of time that just slipped away in the sweet sound and vibration of Om, making the hours we were in the hut melt away seamlessly into a harmony of unity and love for this space and each other. We had become a family unit, sharing our lives together, and now we were vibrating together, at the frequency of the universe, collectively vibrating higher to the cosmic reaches, seeking the knowledge of reality in its purest form.

## Chapter 37

The snowcaps from the Olympic Mountains were almost completely melted. Someone had told me that they had not remembered this ever happening. A few warm summers, some mild winters and global warming have taken some of the charm out of the view from my 68th floor west facing office in downtown Seattle. It was just after my one-year anniversary at this software company, and I was in a leadership role responsible for accounting, finance, HR, operations, IT and project management.

It was a great gig with a ton of responsibility, an office near the top floor in the tallest building in Seattle, facing west over the Puget Sound to the Olympic Mountains. Just 4 ½ years prior I was near death in a hospital from alcoholism. I marveled at the beauty of the spiritual program that allowed me to pick up the shattered mess of my life and return as a functional and happy member of society. Three months prior, I had graduated from business school with an MBA in Executive Management. It was quite an accomplishment and something that I really felt that was earned. I excelled in the program with a perfect 4.0 grade point average. It was an 18 month power drive including two weeks in China of intense international study.

And although I was happy with life, there was still something that was nagging, deep in my subconscious. I recently had become bored with this job and feeling unchallenged, but that wasn't really the truth. If I was going to be rigorously honest with myself, I needed to understand the real reason, because this nagging had been going on for a couple months and it was starting to manifest in my performance.

"Good morning." Dan popped in for a surprise visit. Dan was a happy guy, always with a smile on his jowled face; he walked lightly for a larger guy. His shirts seemed always just a half size too small and his gut hung perfectly over the waistline of straight ironed khakis. Nobody wore ties anymore, especially in Seattle, and a white t-shirt prodded out of the top of the neckline of his blue shirt. I liked him a lot. He brought a down to earth perspective and didn't take life too seriously. As the consultant CFO of the company, he popped in from time to time to see how things were going and was a close advisor to the CEO. I sensed that his presence here today was not jolly. It was 10:00 am on a Monday morning, not a usual time for a visit.

"Got time for a coffee?" This was all he asked. There was a coffee shop on the 40th floor of the building with a panoramic view of Bellevue and the Cascade Mountain range to the East of the city over Lake Washington. At that moment, I knew I was being terminated.

"Sure thing, it's a nice morning for a termination isn't it?" I was beyond the point in my life where I was going to pretend I didn't know what was going on. Although it seemed an odd thing to say, I enjoyed this role, the industry and the people, but I found myself saying it anyway. Dan didn't miss a beat.

"Nothing personal, just a leadership change." He still had a gentle smile on his face and his non-verbal communication told me that there was nothing he could do about it, but also that he wasn't particularly worried about my ability to land on my feet.

We took the elevator down to the 40th floor and Dan went up to the counter to order coffee. I sensed a very relaxed energy from him. In thinking about it, I was the 11th person in this role at the company in the past 12 years so given he had been with the organization for about 7 years, he had done this before.

I found a spot for us to sit and Dan came over with my $6 coffee. Since they were paying, I ordered the large and expensive.

He was completely clean shaven and had soft blue eyes that weren't very penetrating but aware of the details of his surroundings. He had a lot of experience and had transitioned into the role of executive consultant, working when he wanted for whom he wanted. It is nice to be in a position to choose your clients, rather than the other way around. He continued with the conversation that I had abruptly started ahead of schedule up in my office.

"So the CEO has decided to make a leadership change. We are offering you a month of severance for your year of service and you will have to sign both a confidentiality agreement and a waiver of liability."

I sat smiling. This was all standard procedure, the only discussion points being the amount and length of severance and benefits continuation.

"I would like 3 months of insurance coverage. While it has been just over a year of employment, I've spent a considerable amount of hours bringing the accounting system and staffing up to speed. I also think that two months of severance is appropriate. It takes some time to find leadership roles, as you know." I had learned to always ask for more in these situations, and even though this was officially the first job I was ever "fired" from I had been on the other end of the table enough to ask. Dan pondered my request for a moment as he took a sip of coffee.

"I can't do anything about the severance; I had to fight to get you the month. The CEO only offered 2 weeks. The insurance will be no problem." Dan said this with finality in the negotiations. There wasn't much to it, actually. People often want to make these things out to be a dramatic production in their heads when in reality a job termination is usually short and to the point, with little discussion. I had no immediate feeling about the decision one way or the other and accepted it as a chapter that was about to close in my life. We casually strolled from the coffee shop to the elevator to have a quick chat with the CEO about our conversation.

After briefly speaking with the CEO and saying our goodbyes, with the obligatory statements of "it's not being personal" and "we are happy to provide a reference" and "let's do lunch sometime" I packed my office and headed out. I realized that I didn't have many personal effects in my office and I had, over the past several weeks, unconsciously taken a lot of things home already. It was 11:00 am on a Monday morning, an odd time to be terminated. Corporate thought being Friday afternoon is the most optimal time to make staff changes or layoffs because then people have the weekend to burn off the anger or whatever other emotions that are eating them up. The intent there is to prevent workplace violence by having someone come back the very next day or later that day with ill intent. Most people will spend the weekend drinking it off or venting their emotions one way or the other enough that they generate a safe enough distance from the event to not react badly to it. It made me happy that at least they thought I was a stable enough human being that terminating me on a Monday was not a risk.

I walked out the front door of the building onto 4$^{th}$ Avenue to a picture perfect summer day. The sun was reflecting off the tall buildings playing hopscotch on the sidewalk and the air was warm with the smell of salt water wafting up from the Puget Sound below. Rush hour had died down and traffic and the noise from it was at a minimum as I headed north on 4$^{th}$ Ave. Looking at my watch, I realized that I had time to reach the noon yoga class at the studio where I was currently enrolled in teacher training.

The world seemed very surreal on that 10 block walk. I could sense that a great shift was taking place beneath and around me, only I had no identification with it. It was like the world and everything in it was being viewed on a television screen and all of a sudden someone asked me to look at a different television, this one with

147

twice the definition. Things moved in slow, crystal clear motion and for the moment I was completely detached from the universe. I could envision myself in my mind's eye walking up the street, with a yoga mat strapped to my back and a small bag with my personal items from the office. The emotions were completely greyed out and I felt nothing, but saw everything.

A wide eyed homeless person with poor dental work, yellow teeth stained and missing staring at me with hollowness and confusion from the window of a bus; a busy woman in 4" heels bustling by with a cell phone stuck to her ear, so wrapped up in self-image that she almost gets hit by a car; the cracks in the sidewalk, with two small blades of grass growing through the side; a tree's leaves gently swaying in the late morning breeze. The sensory perception of vision and my sixth sense were on overdrive, and I could not hear, smell or taste anything. There was still no emotional attachment to the primary event of the morning. I was standing in front of the yoga studio, not knowing how I arrived. The class was a Vinyasa practice, which turned out to be gentle and nurturing. And while I wasn't really looking for answers as to why I was terminated, at the end of the practice there was a loud and clear message resonating through my being. "Freedom," said the teacher within.

Freedom was nice but it didn't pay the bills. My living standard was at my old salary, not unemployment. It was nice to walk to work but the trade-off was high rent. Tuesday dawned just as nice as Monday and I decided to take a stroll through the neighborhood. To the north, construction cranes filled the skyline with the rise of the Amazon campus, a series of buildings that would house 25,000 employees. Multiple large scale apartment buildings with astronomical rents were also being constructed at a breakneck pace as the real estate developers lined up to cash in on Amazon moving into the South Lake Union neighborhood, which just bordered the downtown corridor, and was once a run-down example of urban plight.

Where drug dealers, prostitutes and homeless once walked the streets, the gentrification of the neighborhood now ensured that software engineers, office managers and web designers would trod from their office to their apartment in back, stopping at the many new retail shops, restaurants and fitness centers that followed. The city would profit greatly from all the new residents and tax revenue, the people who owned the real estate would make a killing in rents with the population density, and people would find out that if they wanted to sacrifice their commute from the suburbs to live downtown, that they also had to sacrifice at least 50% of their after-tax paycheck. It is a hard way to live because of the unbelievable pressure that it puts on simple survival. Given that most people under 35 have a mountain of student loans, it allows for very little disposable income, and no savings. But the alternative is to waste 4 hours a day, 5 days a week in a car moving 5 miles an hour in a line of endless vehicles. Either way, the quality of life suffers. I decided I was done with both.

As I strolled through the neighborhood on this beautiful day, everything was sharp and in extreme focus. The heightened senses and awareness from yesterday were still there, only now the other senses had joined in on the party. There was a distinct awareness of being alive, and I had no idea why I felt this way at this point in time. There were two huge apartment complexes at about 75% completion caddy corner to each other in the back of the neighborhood. As I looked down the small sloping hill towards downtown and the lake I counted another 12 construction cranes and the thought occurred to me that the neighborhood could use a boutique yoga studio.

The combination of business background and yoga teacher training intrigued me. Most of the yoga studio owners I had met struggled with the business aspects and had to learn on the fly and I thought that this would allow me to get the business of the ground faster and reduce the risk of it failing. This thought felt right, like an intention that needed immediate action.

149

The only 'for lease' signs that were available were in the new buildings and I shuddered to think what the rent was for that space. I knew two very important points about starting a business and I intended to practice both of them: minimize upfront investment and minimize fixed overhead cost, such as rent. I returned home to search the internet for below market space. A yoga studio could be built into any space and I believed that location and the quality of the building was secondary given the cost trade off necessary for market rate rent. I also believed that utilizing an older building would give the space some charm and not have the sterile feel of a new building. New construction is boilerplate and lacks energy.

On Wednesday a meeting was scheduled with the real estate agent for an older building across the street from the two major apartment construction sites. It was 1,200 square feet of open space, enough to put a small practice room in that would hold about 20 people. It felt perfect. The theory was that people would look at the outside building and see a 50-year-old structure, in need of some repair, and then walk into the space and see the beautiful transformation of what had been built inside. This was a beautiful yogic metaphor and how the space would be viewed and it was the first impression that I wanted the student to realize when entering the space. The rate for the space was less than 5 times the going market rate, which would be a critical competitive advantage if I could secure the lease and get the business off the ground.

I arrived at the building at 10:00 am on Wednesday, and it struck me odd that two days earlier I was in a high profile corporate job in the tallest building in Seattle and now I was looking to rent a tiny space in a run-down building in an up and coming neighborhood, starting a business in an industry I knew nothing about. "Trust God, faith and the teacher within," I kept saying to myself. It felt right, and instead of allowing the fear of the unknown overcome me, I intended to march forward, come what may. The space was perfect and I arranged a meeting with the landlord the following day. He would not sign a lease with anyone he had not met in person. I liked that I would be dealing with an individual rather than a corporation.

Thursday morning I headed down to the coffee shop a block from the apartment to meet the owner of the building. I was asked to prepare a statement of my financial condition and a plan for the business and it occurred to me that I didn't really have a financial condition.

Even almost five years into sobriety, financial recovery was still in process. I lived paycheck to paycheck and had a severance package and meager savings to my name. I did have a plan, however, and with the low rent and me being the primary teacher at the studio, costs would be low which meant that it would require a relatively small number of customers to cover the expenses of the business. The landlord William introduced himself when I entered the shop. He was slim and looked to be in good shape for a man in his 60s. He moved with ease as he approached me to shake hands. A hat covered his balding head and he had a short gray beard. Despite being an obviously wealthy man given that he owned a prime piece of real estate in downtown Seattle, one could not tell this from neither his appearance nor his mannerisms. He was quiet and humble in his approach.

"Nice to meet you, can I get you a coffee?" He asked as we shook hands. I liked his energy and thought about how this was something that I noticed now. In my old sense of self, when I met a new person my only feelings were of fear of whether or not I would be accepted by the person I was meeting, and now it didn't matter to me. My mind was trained to think that the other person's opinion of me was none of my business. It was yet more proof of how much change had occurred, and the awareness of that change.

"Nice to meet you, just a decaf drip, thank you." I was trying to minimize coffee intake due to caffeine sensitivity. After we exchanged some additional pleasantries and background information I took some time to explain the business idea and financial situation. After he was satisfied with the description of the idea, he looked at me over the rims of his glasses, which had been studying one of the spreadsheets that were on the table in front of him.

"I like the idea; the neighborhood can use this. I am very concerned about your ability to finance the business operations and build-out costs. As you know the building is old, and I do not provide any costs for build-out as part of the lease. Also, any lease includes a clause that states that I can redevelop the land at any point in time, which means you will lose the space. In reality, the zoning takes 1-2 years minimum, so take that into account." He was reading my non-verbal body language and communicating very intently as he said this. I liked his open and frank attitude; it was refreshing in a business world gone astray with roundabout communication designed to eliminate any personal responsibility.

"What are the redevelopment plans?" I asked this because if he had any specific plans in place the business took on a much different look. I was confident it would turn a profit, but also knew that it may take a year or two to get to that stage and probably three to four years before I saw any return on my investment, financially anyway. I saw far greater benefit in the lifestyle this would afford me by taking me out of corporate America, which had caused me so much internal conflict, and into a role where I was both teaching and helping people grow, which I thought was more in line with my true calling in life. It almost didn't seem like work.

"The rent from the building is income for my Great Aunt. When she passes, we will most likely redevelop or sell and redevelop." He took a sip of his coffee and glanced idly around the room as he said this. The people in the coffee shop were too self-absorbed to notice anyone so he brought his attention back to me. I could see that he already knew my question, which I was trying to phrase as politely as possible.

"Do you mind me asking how old she is?" I said this sheepishly as I didn't want to offend the man and his dear Great Aunt!

"She is 95 and in perfect health!" He said this with a flourish like she had just finished her third marathon this year. I wasn't surprised by this actually because he was well into his 60's and was in great physical condition.

We finished up our conversation and later that afternoon he sent me a lease to sign. Nine years with a few months of abated rent upfront. Build-out was entirely up to me. I signed the lease and handed over my entire severance package for the deposit and first month's rent, completely on faith. However, not blind faith. Blind faith without discernment and the application of intelligence is stupidity, in particular on financial decisions that have high amounts of risk associated with them.

I had faith that I could get the business off the ground, but needed two things to make that happen. Financing and permits from the city. I asked and received a clause in the lease that said if those two things could not be attained in the next 90 days that the lease was void and it would cost me half my security deposit. So I risked a couple of thousand dollars on my ability to make this happen, and given my financial situation, it was like taking most of my life savings, walking into a casino and betting it on one blackjack hand.

The only difference being that my faith was on my skill and ability to make this happen being better than my faith at playing one hand of high stakes blackjack. To celebrate the signing of the lease I went to a yoga class and stopped and ate a spinach salad on the way home with an organic fruit juice. Celebrating in sobriety and living a healthy life; so much had changed.

On Friday it was time to get to work. Sitting in the same coffee shop where I had met the landlord, I must have looked very out of place sitting alone at a table with a huge smile on my face. It is rare to see people genuinely smile, especially in coffee shops where for some reason people are trying hard to look very important. I still had no idea how in four days I went from corporate executive to unemployed to yoga studio owner with a nine-year lease. It also occurred to me that I still had two months left before I was officially a *yoga teacher*. The voice inside me kept prodding me along, reassuring me that I was on the right path, and that continuing to listen was important. I was listening, and the signal was loud and clear!

My intention was to build a yoga studio with the ability for heated classes. While this was the more expensive option, there was only one shot at the build-out, so it had to be planned and executed correctly. Business planning was a strength. Construction projects and getting permits from the city were not only a weakness, they were completely new territory. My strategy was to minimize the mistakes that I knew I would make and not beat the hell out of myself when I made them. My budget for the build-out with gross numbers showed $25,000 was needed. This didn't count operating expenses once the studio was open to cover losses or the cost of my living expenses during the time it was constructed. It was also imperative that the remodel happen as quickly as possible so that I was still in the free rent period when the studio opened. My hope was that I would teach most of the classes avoiding teacher pay at first. Other than that, the studio was relatively inexpensive to operate. Monthly internet and supplies for ambiance and cleaning were about all that was needed. I would learn later there was more, mostly in one-time costs, and also learn the difficulty of customer retention in a short attention span world.

I also knew that the business would afford some nice tax breaks that all small business owners enjoyed. As this worked through my mind, the phone rang. It was Vic who was a classmate from graduate school at Washington State University. He lived in Portland and worked at a large athletic apparel company, in fact, the largest one in the world. We became good friends and even though the EMBA program was mostly online, we spent two weeks in China together in the international immersion part of the program. He was in town for his wedding anniversary and wanted to get together. It was a beautiful day outside so we decided to meet at an Irish pub down on the waterfront.

"Who the hell would fire you?" was Vic's first question when I informed him of the recent job change. He was an athlete, a tri-athlete to be exact. He was junior to me by about five years, well built and light brown hair that was just beginning to gray around the edges. He had a calm demeanor that served him well in his leadership role in a large organization that required the ability to deal with multiple and sometimes extreme personality types. The sun was behind him silhouetting his tall and broad shouldered frame that took up too much of the plastic chair at our outdoor table.

"Exactly what I was thinking. I am pretty amazing, far too amazing to actually fire. My immediate thought was to barge into the CEO's office and inform her that I couldn't be fired – I was sober! They didn't know about that, though. But the reality is I had mentally checked out of the role. Something was bugging me and even though I couldn't put a finger on it, it was affecting my performance, or at the very least, my enthusiasm for the day to day grind there. I was still doing the job, but it was quite an effort." He was completely supportive of my logic and explanation, and there was no concern on his part that I would land on my feet. He took a sip of a choice IPA from his pint glass.

"That is one thing I don't deal with; it is really hard to get canned from my company. Have you considered reaching out to our network from university for job networking? We have that group formed on the link up website." I could see the wheels turning in his head on what he could do to support the process. It was very kind.

"I know what you mean, when I worked at that huge software company that moved me out here, it was almost impossible to get canned. Of course I figured out a way to basically get managed out of the role there, but I was drinking a case of beer a day then." I took a sip of my near beer and marveled at how it tastes very much like beer but without the alcohol. A lot of people in AA frowned upon drinking near beer, but I didn't see any harm in it. I enjoyed the taste and it gave me a sense of normalcy when I was out with people in bar and restaurant environments. It also lessened the need for me to explain to people why I didn't drink because most people aren't aware enough to notice that the beer is non-alcoholic. He took a glance at his phone. Vic had two daughters that were 12 and 10 and they were back in Portland while he and his wife celebrated 15 years of marriage here in Seattle. They were staying at one of the nicer hotels downtown.

"So what are you planning to do?" he asked this while browsing the menu, his white freckled skin starting to get a little pink from the sun.

"I signed a 9 year lease yesterday on a space in South Lake Union to open a yoga studio. I gave the landlord my entire severance package. I have no money to do the build-out or to open the business, and no idea how to build it and even further no idea how to get the permits. That being said, it feels right. It is like the universe **wants** this to happen. I also wasn't an idiot about it. If I can't get the financing or the permits, I can get out of the lease with only a couple thousand in penalties."

He laughed out loud. It was a reassuring and supporting show of emotion. "You got it man. Whatever "it" is, you got it. Your attitude, and I noticed this in grad school, is anything can be done by anyone with the right mindset. Happy for you and I am confident that it will work out." I started laughing at his confidence where I was starting to think I may need to rent a padded room.

"Vic, I have come to believe, ah scratch that, have faith in the human condition. At least my human condition. Change and making things happen in this world come in three easy steps that are incredibly difficult to execute. So much to overcome in the human mind. Willingness, a belief that it can be done and then taking the actions necessary to get it done. This has been the formula for change since man walked out of a cave. I certainly have the willingness; I am done being an employee in Corporate America. I don't think I like having bosses. I have faith in spades, and that has come from getting sober, learning music and getting the MBA and all the other experiences that I've earned once I got sober.

You know Vic; addiction is such an interesting study. One thing that addicts share is this concept of the earning principle being short circuited. We want everything now and we want it supersized because when we put alcohol or drugs in our body it immediately solves our emotional problem, and we then translate that into the rest of our life. That is one reason why addicts become such a pain in the ass as the disease worsens. The earning principle is broken, even if it was installed in early childhood. My parents taught me very well the earning principle and I have never been afraid of hard work, but through my addiction it had gotten short circuited. Everything I have done in sobriety has not only corrected this, but added the beauty of gratitude to the equation." Even though Vic didn't have addiction affecting his life, he always paid rapt attention when I talked about the topic. It fascinated him.

"And the action items? That seems the most daunting of the three to me because it requires the most effort. The first two seem to be mental exercises." The sun was beginning to dip completely behind him as the afternoon came to that beautiful hour or two

157

before the sunset, where the day seemed to freeze as the city took a deep breath after a long day of work. It occurred to me the beautiful human connection that Vic and I had and how that had been unavailable to me during my drinking career.

"To be certain, and often our own ignorance keeps us from knowing the action items. But without the first two steps, we are dead in the water, whether they are mental exercises or not. The action items are the devil in the details. But frankly, I like simplification. The world has gone and gotten over complicated, and in my opinion, it is because people like to complicate things for the gratification of their giant egos and then waste the world's time with their complications. To me, the steps of how to do anything are usually laid out in front of us if we are willing to stop for a minute and think about it. And not necessarily in a linear fashion. This is a major fault in Western thinking and causes a lot of dependencies to happen on a project which creates delays in delivery. But independent of that, what I see people doing is looking at the totality of a project and they convince themselves that it can't be done. If I look at financing, getting permits and building a yoga studio in its totality, I am going to get bogged down in the enormity of it and nothing will happen." The waiter came by and interrupted and we ordered a couple of appetizers and another round of beer. Vic was a smart guy and knew exactly where I was coming from. He continued my thought process for me.

"I run into this at work on large scale IT projects. We will be replacing an entire data center, which is a huge project, not so much because of the hardware replacement, but ensuring that there is no downtime for the servers that are doing the work. This is no small task given even with the built in redundancy. We project plan it down to minutia on a timeline. You know, standard project management. I often wondered why people don't apply the same thought process to their lives." The waiter brought another round of beers and he took a sip while I continued.

"Lack of training. Life skills aren't taught these days. But even with that there is another major stumbling block. Lack of knowledge. On this project, I have no idea how to get city permits and little to no idea on construction, which I intend to do myself with the exception of electrical work. But I am handy and have been fixing things all my life and know enough to know that when I don't know something, to do the research or ask someone who does. I imagine the internet can steer me through a lot of this too, especially on the permits. In any event, it will work out exactly as it is supposed to one way or the other." With that part of the conversation coming to a close, a weird thought popped into my mind and before I actually had a chance to process the thought, it came out of my mouth. "And by the way, if your company needs any consultants, I imagine that I have 60 to 90 days of free time before I can acquire the permits to complete the build-out." I said this rather offhandedly with no expectations and in fact, Vic had no reaction at all so I wasn't sure if he even heard me. He had just finished an onion ring and looked up; his sunglasses now perched on top of his head.

"Do you know a place that has good burgers? My wife and I are looking for a good burger for dinner." I thought that was an odd request for an anniversary dinner. I gave him a couple of recommendations and we said our goodbyes. It was almost time for the annual WSU football game in Seattle and we promised to get together for that in a couple of months.

On Saturday morning I met the landlord at the space to do the walkthrough and to get the keys. The walkthrough was a formality as I was taking the space as is. The entry had a wrought iron gate with an apse that had the main door. The gate was there to keep the homeless from sleeping on the stoop. It would need to be removed and the primary door would need to be moved out to the street. This would also increase the usable square footage on the inside.

The space was a big, empty room with two small bathrooms in the corner. The cinder block walls that shared the outside of the building were painted an acrid dark yellow and the one common wall with the neighboring office was painted off white that was stained to yellow after many years of neglect. The carpeting was at least 30 years old and would need to be replaced with a subfloor and then whatever flooring was chosen for the studio. The ceiling was dropped and also 30 years old. The demo work required was daunting just to get the space into shape for build-out. The landlord left me to my own devices without saying much and I found a seat in the middle of the room. And I sat. Quietly and patiently, emptying my mind to listen to the teacher within. I sat there in silence for three hours. The planning process was underway.

On Monday morning, the process of understanding how to permit a business began. I had taken the day off on Sunday from all thoughts of the studio and how to get this done. A mental break had been in order. I figured most of the information was available on the web as Seattle was a very web centric and technological city, and this assumption was correct. I needed a "Change of Use" permit which allowed me to change the space from "Office Space" to "Gym and Athletic Space". It was required that plans for the build-out be submitted and approved. This was all a nice way for the city to collect some tax revenue on the business before it even opened. The permit process was not nearly as complicated as I anticipated but the cost was higher. Score one point for going over budget on the first item researched. As I began to meander the internet to yoga studio flooring my phone started ringing. It was Vic.

"Hey Vic, how was the rest of the anniversary weekend in Seattle? Find that burger joint?" One of the burger places was actually in his hotel.

"We decided on steak. It was nice, a great weekend. I don't have much time as I am about to run into a meeting but I wanted to let you know that I have a 90-day consulting opportunity for you here in Portland if you don't mind being down here three days a week. We can pay you a fixed rate for the entire project. If you get done early, so be it. I think the project is right in your wheelhouse given your background. We need someone to validate a major IT project that we started a year ago. A lot of complex spreadsheet modeling, ROI, contracts, etc. We don't have anyone in house that can do it because they have all moved to different teams within the company so we need someone who can get up to speed fast, recreate and validate the initial assumptions, and then report on where we are at against the initial project plan and also recommend any course corrections. You will be on my team and the company will cover your travel expenses back and forth. When you are in Seattle, you can work from your home office. I gotta run, think about it and give me a ring later this afternoon." And with that he hung up.

My email inbox pinged a second later and it had the rate of pay for the project. My jaw dropped. In one week I had gone from corporate executive to Yoga studio owner looking for a way to build and finance a yoga studio to corporate consultant at the largest sports apparel company in the world. And the pay for the 90-day contract covered the entire cost of the studio plus living expenses. It did not cover initial working capital by initial estimates but what a start. I sat quietly for a moment and felt gratitude swell in my heart and permeate my existence, and the grace of God that followed brought me to tears.

I could feel the bigger picture and begin to see it in my mind. The purpose, or Dharma of my life, was finally coming to pass. I spent so much time lost in a foggy haze of alcohol driven by the confusion of self, my ignorance and ego and primarily not understanding the rules of life. I had ignored them for so long because of a childish petulance sprung from this ignorance, and complete paralysis driven by irrational fears created by high sensitivity. I poured alcohol on this fire of emotions until it burned so hot that it almost consumed my soul. I could now see why I was saved. I asked the question to myself so many times. Why me?

My sponsor Clive had told me not to worry about the why. It wasn't important. Maybe not, but another dear friend and sponsor for a short time before Clive reminded me that true faith is knowing that eventually everything will make sense, borrowing the quote from Vaclav. I had discernment from the question which allowed me to stay a safe enough distance from it that it didn't consume my being. This discernment allowed me to see the bigger picture.

My Dharma, and the reason I was saved, was to teach spirituality using the tool of Yoga and my life experience as a drunk and in recovery to help others to grow. The ones that sought it anyway. We always say in AA that the program is for those who want it, not for those who need it. When I felt grace, there were no words to describe its beauty. It is like the hand of the divine reaching down and kissing your soul, giving you the briefest glimpse of the eternal bliss within. It is the ultimate peace and feeling it, even if for a nanosecond, brings the hope, courage and strength to move mountains. It encourages me, that in a world of madness, there is good, and it is within every human being, we just have to open our eyes and look *beyond* our senses to see it.

I emailed Vic back in ten minutes. I wanted to at least give him the impression that I made a well thought out decision. Later that afternoon he got back to me, I started the following Monday.

On Tuesday afternoon after spending sometime meditating in the studio about design, I was pouring through the mail and got an envelope from the Washington State University. I opened it and inside was a rather sizable check refunding me for the last session that I was in graduate school. I had paid the tuition out of pocket rather than through loans. In speaking with my tax attorney and having her inform me that I was free to do with the money as I

162

pleased, so long as it was repaid, I decided to put it towards the Yoga studio project.

On Thursday afternoon the business attorney that I used for consulting matters gave me a ring. For years I had supplemented my income with part time consulting gigs. I had an outstanding dispute with a client that was over a year old and I had no expectation of ever getting paid. The client made a settlement offer for 60% of what was due. I agreed to put the matter behind me.

*Monday - Terminated, acquired freedom*

*Tuesday - Decided on Yoga Studio*

*Wednesday - Found Space*

*Thursday - Signed Lease*

*Friday - Chatted with Vic on consulting*

*Monday - Offered Consulting*

*Tuesday - Received WSU Check*

*Thursday - Received Settlement from old Client*

*Do Good, Do Dharma, Trust the Universe*

On a small sheet of paper on my desk I had written the events of the past two weeks. I wasn't sure if I believed it myself. But it was at that moment in time that Ripple Yoga was born. I chose Ripple Yoga simply because of the belief that the way we change the world is one person at a time, ourselves. And by changing ourselves we inspire others to do the same.

This is the *Ripple Effect,* and I specifically wanted to create a ripple effect in humanity by helping people change themselves. Positive change happens in the world through spiritual growth and evolution, not through fear, anger, hatred and ignorance.

We are born with what Patanjali in the Yoga Sutras calls Kleshas, and these are characteristics that are built into the human condition, many of them which are left over from the older animal part of our brain. They are inborn, so there isn't anything we can do about them other than to work on them with our higher mind. The Kleshas are ignorance, ego, likes, dislikes and our survival instinct. In order for us to evolve and grow spiritually, we must overcome or go beyond our Kleshas. What this means is that we must learn to control them with the higher part of the mind, the human part of our mind, the neo-cortex. We often hear the term "subjugate the ego" which literally means to put the ego in the back seat and to not allow it to control our thought process and subsequent behaviors. It means to respond and to not react.

Most of the problems in the world today and throughout human history have been caused by ignorance, which can be defined as the inability to see reality. Ignorance creates and drives fear, and human history is littered with examples of it. Hitler's Germany, slavery in America, the Crusades. Ignorance, which is perceived through a misperception in our senses, tells us that **those** people are different, and therefore they are a threat, perceived or real. Ignorance allows us to see duality when the universe and our higher self-desires unity.

An example of this is when we are working and one of our coworkers who we have been friends with for years is suddenly promoted ahead of us. We are unable to see the reasons for the promotion and our ignorance, or inability to see reality, starts to drive fear into us in the form of jealousy. Our survival instinct suddenly kicks in because we perceive a threat to our security. Suddenly our coworker is earning more money and we had already planned on being in that role. In our mind, we had already spent the raise we were never assured of getting in the first place. How can we live at our current income level? Never mind that we have been living happily on it for six years. Our ego starts to tell us that we were more deserving, throwing judgment into the mix. Our ego starts to tell us that our coworker probably cheated somehow to get the promotion. Suddenly we decide that we never really liked that person much anyway.

And from this simple business decision we are filled with multiple forms of fear, start performing poorly at our existing job, and end up getting released four months down the road for poor performance. We then blame our coworker who got the promotion for our termination, the same coworker who we were close friends with for the past six years since arriving at the company. Our mind is then filled with poison and resentment for the person, the company and not to mention the ill effects of all this on the people that love us and have to live with us on a daily basis.

The spiritually awakened individual, one who is part of the ripple effect, seeks to understand the decision of the coworker being promoted and does not emotionally react. They take a moment to breathe because there is an understanding that the senses lie to us and that our sensory perception of the world is through the filters of both the senses and the Kleshas. This person develops an objective distance from the event and understands that the person got promoted simply because they were better suited for the role and accepts that there is more work to do, more improving in their skill set before they are rewarded. This person saves themselves, their family and the friendship with the coworker by simply being aware of themselves and how the human being is built.

# Chapter 38

I slipped out of the ashram into the semi darkness of dusk at 6:15. We weren't supposed to leave the ashram after 6:00 because of pending darkness, but from time to time I enjoyed the short walk to the corner store. It was a very warm evening signaling that the brutal South Indian heat of the spring was just around the corner. To the right I could hear the gentle lapping of the waves of the Bay of Bengal against the shoreline about 300 yards down the narrow road.

To the left the poorly kept and potholed road stretched about 500 yards to a dead end. Small houses and huts were on either side of the road and the school children were just making their way home from the day's classes, their playful chatter ringing through the late afternoon sunset. Mothers stood out on doorsteps talking to neighbors and herding the children in for dinner while fathers were arriving home on scooters from their day job. This was just another day in India, people living their lives, chasing their dreams, fulfilling their Dharma.

I strolled down the road to the store in bare feet. It occurred to me that in the five months since arriving, I hardly ever wore shoes of any kind and if I did they were open toed sandals. That was the culture here and the connection to the earth through bare feet, especially in India with its rich history and virtue, had a feeling to it that was different from other places in the world. Walking barefoot in the West was like walking through a sterilized hospital wing. There is no feeling other than the cold of the floor. Here I could feel the history and the vibration of the lifestyle through the soles of the feet. I could feel the adults coming home from work as children playing in

166

these same streets, their smiles and laughter vibrating up from the ground as a permanent beauty.

As I reached the end of the street I could turn left or right. To the right was the small local temple, complete with 10 to 15 goats. I had watched five goats from birth and named them. The single brown one was named Curtis. Then there were two pairs; Pepe and Jorge, the Spanish twins, and Stan and Laurel, named after the American comedians. One day when I was petting Curtis, the owner of the goats offered him to me to ride around on my bicycle. Today I would be turning left to head out to the main road and the store.

The road ran another 300 yards with small huts and houses on the right, the huts with the common coconut tree leaf roofing and the houses the squat colorful concrete variety, usually one room. On the right was a small field with a tree which usually housed four cows. One of the cows I had named Fred and since he was always stumbling across the main road and back and forth from the beach in a very haphazard manner, I gave him a backstory. Fred had a drinking problem, and his brother Earl was trying to get him into rehab. Once all four cows were lying in the field and it looked like an intervention for poor Fred!

When walking down the roads barefoot in India, it is very common that feces from cows, goats, chickens, dogs, cats and all other walks of life is strewn about the road. It dries and it is swept around, and in particular the cow dung is absorbed through the feet providing very necessary and beneficial probiotics for human beings. Walking barefoot through cow dung would be frowned upon in the West, and it made me chuckle.

What is commonplace here is considered filthy in the West. Walking barefoot in most places in the West is unhealthy because of all the chemicals and manmade materials spilled in our streets and used to pollute our lawns under the guise of sterility.

167

In India, it is nature meeting nature. But in our rush to judgment, clouded by our own ignorance of how the world is, and refusal to accept that there may be, just maybe another way, we immediately look down our noses in disdain at other cultures and label them as "bad". We act oh so self-righteous in the judgment, our giant over inflated egos on full display.

And this inability to see beyond anything but our very limited experience cripples our growth. We approach everything with that same closed mind because of an irrational fear that maybe; just maybe we are wrong about something.

I smiled as I continued down the road and found gratitude in the fact that I cherished being wrong, because when I was wrong, I immediately learned something and expanded my consciousness.

Everything in our life is put there by the Universe as a learning opportunity, and we are given a choice every minute of every day to either learn something, or to ignore it and continue our life in ignorance, blinded by the irrationality of fear, stunted by the overburden of likes and dislikes, and limited by our ego.

And from these internal sources, we find misery, and we don't understand why we are unhappy, so we start blaming the world and the people, places and things in the world for our misery and unhappiness. Some of us, so few but some of us recognize that maybe, just maybe, we are wrong, and that realization opens the door to growth. We begin to see that we are in charge of our happiness, not anyone else. We begin to see that we have a choice to be happy every minute of every day. We begin to take responsibility for own lives.

# Chapter 39

"Nice final report, great meeting."  Vic was smiling in his office in Portland, OR. It was time to head back to Seattle, the project was successfully completed.  The timing of the universe was starting to baffle me, as the construction permit for the Yoga studio was issued on the exact same day as the project was finished in Portland. Vic and I said our goodbyes and I made the three-hour journey back north to Seattle to build a Yoga studio into an empty office space, without the slightest idea of how to do so.

On and off over the past month of the sporting apparel company project, I was confident enough in the permit being eventually approved by the city that I was able to do a fair amount of the demolition work, including removing the carpet and the ceiling. It was an incredibly messy job with too many trips to the dump to count. I had estimated that stuffing my 15-year-old beater SUV to the gills with construction trash was cheaper than hiring a company to haul it away.

It was a flat fee to dump in an ordinary vehicle.  I moved forward with the construction learning on the fly, utilizing the internet, asking people and making mistakes. I hired an electrician, handyman to guide me and help on trickier parts and a guy to help hang drywall. The flooring, tiling, painting, wall framing, and finishing work I did myself, with an incredible savings in labor on the project.

The electrician went over budget, materials went under budget, labor was on budget, and flooring and heaters were on budget.  After all was said and done, the studio build-out was completed for $2,000 over budget, or about 8%. I was quite proud of myself, having never budgeted this type of project.

After working 16 hours a day, 7 days a week the studio opened 45 days from the start of the build-out. I was shocked that it only took 45 days to completely transform the space. And in the first two weeks of classes, all of which I taught, four people showed up. Four total people across sixteen classes. Granted, it was the holidays, but four people seemed quite abysmal. And for the first two weeks that the studio was open, all the classes were free! I decided to not charge for classes until January 1, 2014, which is what is now considered the opening date.

Disheartened was not a strong enough word to explain what I was feeling. I needed to constantly remind myself that the universe wanted this. I also spent those first two weeks in December distributing flyers around the neighborhood and trying to get the website traction in the wild and overcrowded world of the internet. In January, people slowly started to attend the practices. I brought on two teachers that were in teacher training with me and a full schedule of 20 classes a week.

Near the end of January, I was sitting in the foyer where students signed in pondering this new lifestyle and career, and the beauty of what had been created. The outside of the building, which had been dingy tan when the lease was signed, was now a vibrant blue, in line with the colors of the logo that was chosen for the business. Ripple Yoga was emblazoned in white across the brick façade with concentric circles in purple, grey and light blue making up the "O" in Yoga. A clear fiberglass awning curved like a circle arc hung over the old fashioned wooden door that served as the new entryway. The door had a glass insert which had an open/close sign on it. Two windows looked into the quaint space and one window adorned a chalkboard with the current class schedule.

When students came into the space, they were greeted with a warm white with just a hint of tinted blue running down a long wall in front of them moving left to the doorway to the practice room. To the right was a small area where people checked in at a retail stand facing a lighter blue wall, again consistent with the logo. Dark blue glass coned torch lamps hung from 4 foot cords with halogen bulbs lighting the common area of the studio.

At the other end of the hallway was a set of cubbies where students could leave their mats. The floors were a grey ceramic with dark grout, nicely matching the logo and the overall color scheme. Three tan area rugs made of hemp adorned the floor keeping the feet warm in the winter months.

The practice room was about 24 feet by 16 feet and had the same door as the entry to the studio. The floor was a bright blue that looked like the ocean and the walls were a light grey with light blue tint. With the lights low in the room, the floors and walls ran together giving a serene and gentle feel to the practice space. Five small one foot square windows were placed in the room to allow natural light in and depending on the day, sunlight would stream in creating shadows and shapes on the walls, sometimes looking like it was raining in through a prism. The room had an amazing and beautiful energy that many people commented on after their practice.

And while I pondered the beauty of the space, I also had to face the reality of it as a business. And as is usual with a new business, the revenue projection was out of line with reality. Despite having a significant advantage on cost structure, the studio struggled mightily for the first six months and it required constant capital infusion to stay afloat. I was the source of the capital infusion and was running out of money. By the end of January, the studio was broke. It became apparent that I was going to have to find some additional consulting work in order to keep the business alive and to pay my personal expenses.

I had already moved into a cheaper apartment saving about $600 a month. But faith and fulfilling one's Dharma is an amazing process. The universe wanted this to happen. It was an exercise in trusting the Divine and the will of the Divine, of this I was sure. In Yoga, it was called an exercise in **Isvara Pranidana**. In AA, it was following the third step, almost to the letter. As I sat waiting for students to show up for a 5:30 PM Vinyasa class and realizing that payroll was going to be $400 short for the coming Friday, I was pondering this. Having no access to bank capital or other forms of loan, I questioned my faith. This is where the rubber hits the road on faith.

There is a certain turning point where we are faced with reality, and reality seems bleak. Did I make a huge mistake in opening the space? Surely the financial planning and revenue projections were off, but it was only a month open and already struggling. What was the lesson here? I had learned repeatedly that everything that happens in life is tied to a lesson to help us burn karma. When it came to what AA calls 'fear of financial insecurity' I had it in spades. I started to panic with 15 minutes left before class.

The feelings of uselessness and pain welled up inside me. I couldn't control the damaging emotional train running downhill from my ego to my heart, looking to crush all faith in its path. I felt worthless, even in the evidence of the beautiful space that surrounded me, the space that I had built. When in this space, all that had been accomplished during five years of sobriety and all spiritual growth went out the window. I became a scared child, filled with 1,000 irrational fears gnawing at the fiber of my being.

Each fear came at me from a different angle causing me to cower into an emotional ball. The ego was in full assault of the higher self, its loudspeakers blaring from the rooftops the tortuous truth. "I told you this wouldn't work!" "You could have stayed in Corporate America and would have been very comfortable financially! You have no business teaching anything. Who wants to learn from a drunk? You can barely take care of yourself, how can you be responsible for something like this? Why don't you just give up and pack it in?"

It all felt like the truth. My heart ached with this reality and my head drooped forward into my hands. I gave up. This was it. I would inform the teachers that I couldn't pay them and that I would wind down operations. The bitterness of this reality turned my blood to acid, poisoning my emotions, sapping my energy and wilting my soul. I could feel the flame of hope dying in me, this small dream burning up before my eyes.

I looked up and there were two people standing in front of me smiling, signing in for the practice. They had come to practice a week before. Initially the new student special was the first class for free. I had put 20 class cards on sale for $229 and each of them happily purchased a 20 class card, telling me how happy they were with a small neighborhood yoga studio across the street from their apartment and how much they enjoyed my teaching style.

As they walked away to go into the practice room, I looked at the number in the sales register: $458. I guess we will make payroll after all. Starting a business that is undercapitalized is a daily struggle, even with all the business knowledge in the world. Even with the known risk factors managed appropriately, customers can be fickle, the systemic risk of recession and other external forces of nature can adversely affect the success of the operation.

Ripple Yoga struggled along mightily for the first 18 months, so much so that I took a part time consulting role to subsidize the business. The studio became a labor of love, and not something done for profit. Over the first 18 months of operations, I taught about

1,500 Yoga classes to over a thousand students, and spent another 20 hours a week on managing the studio which included the website, all email and other marketing, hiring and managing the teaching staff and ensuring that the space was maintained, supplied and cleaned. For this effort, I received exactly zero dollars of pay and in fact invested 80% of my pretax consulting income into the business to keep it afloat. I lived meagerly. Many people asked me why I would work 60 hours a week to support a business that didn't make money. The answer was simple and straightforward. It was my Dharma, all of the work associated with the studio was not work to me, and it was my responsibility to provide this to the community. Those are the internal factors of human responsibility, or Dharma, which are important to living a virtuous life. It taught me **Aparigrahah**, or non-greed, the 5$^{th}$ of the Yamas. It taught me to let go of any fear of financial insecurity, as we say in AA. It taught me that my *work* could be an act of Karma Yoga, teaching others, with no expectation of anything in return.

But nothing in life is free, but for the grace of God, and that was returned to me like the ocean washing away the daily debris on the seashore, leaving the morning fresh and new and the sun rising to glisten off a clean beach. When a student comes to me after class and thanks me because they have had a bad day and the message that was carried to them in practice made a difference in their life, and I could feel their gratitude wash over my being, that made it worth every moment of frustration. I felt myself vibrating at a higher plane of existence, above the greed and selfishness of the world and in this space lays the happiness that is so sought after. It is in this virtue, and the seeking of this virtue, where happiness exists. Letting go of the social conditioning, or Samskara, that everything has to be done for something in return, even in the business world, allowed another step in the freeing of the soul from the eternal disease of rebirth.

# Chapter 40

It is said that that practice of Yoga will make us more efficient. This can be extended to the practice of spiritualty. As my accomplishments in sobriety, which to me was the same as saying accomplishments on the spiritual path began to pile up; it amazed me what could be done by applying these principles, in what seemed like very little time. At first I credited it to not spending umpteen hours a day drunk or in a bar, and to an extent this was true.

But to a greater extent it was the ability or flow created by applying the principles of the AA program or Yama/Niyama in the Yogic world in my life. I began to see through **Swadiyaya** that the practice of right use with the right people at the right time had a strange way of twisting time in my favor. The word 'accomplishments' seems shallow and the reality is the accomplishments that became available by the type of person that I was becoming. By living and fulfilling my Dharma, my responsibilities were increasing but the ability to fulfill those responsibilities increased as well. It was as if the universe was managing things in a very efficient manner for me so long as I stayed on my Dharmic path.

I dragged a brand new guitar 10,000 miles to India with very little idea how to play it. For the first two months of the trip it sat in the corner of the room staring at me, wondering if it would ever get the opportunity to be played. During the rainy season, the humidity and moisture rusted the strings so I replaced them. Something inside me around Christmastime told me to pick it up and play it every day for just an hour or two, enough to get the callouses built up on the fingers and a basic idea of the strum pattern. I had enough music theory in me from five years of piano lessons to last me this lifetime, so understanding the functionality of the instrument was little problem. I remember telling my music teacher during piano lessons that there was no way that I could ever catch up to all the theory that he had taught me.

And sure enough, each time I sit down at the piano I am sifting through one of the lessons trying to apply it, to gain the wisdom of the experience of playing from the theory. One thing is for certain, memorizing theory from a book is relatively useless in life without finding a way to apply it. Once applied, it becomes learned, and once it is applied, it becomes wisdom, as knowledge plus the experience is just that. This had been my mantra over the past few years. Learn something, and then figure out a way to apply it.

This guitar staring at me from the corner of the room in the ashram was no different. So I just started to play it. I forced myself to play a couple songs on Christmas for everyone and they were recorded. It was just short of horrible, but the instrument was in use, and there was singing along with it. Soon after, it was played during Bajans.

I then downloaded music from the internet and the pieces began to fall into place. We become adept and skillful in life by learning and applying learning through experience and practice, but the foundation has to be in place. For me to play the guitar, some of the foundation was in place. I knew how to read music. I understood the theory of scale, the circle of fifths, rhythm and how the guitar functioned as an instrument. I could tune it by ear. The only piece missing was picking it up and going through the uncomfortable process of sucking at it long enough to become capable of playing it. And that is where a major stumbling block lies. There is a fear of doing something poorly so it becomes a non-starter in our endeavors. Growth in human existence has always followed the same formula. We have a willingness to change. We then believe that we can change. We then take the action steps necessary to change.

Willingness, belief and action. If any one of those three components is missing change cannot occur.

When I was drinking myself to death, for a long time there was no willingness to change. There was also no belief. But eventually through being sick enough, and reaching a tipping point where a literal life or death decision needed to be made, I decided that by a very slim margin I was willing to change, to quit drinking. That saved my life. My higher self or greater good from within saved my entire self. At that point I had no belief that a life of sobriety could exist, but I was told that I didn't need to worry about that and just worry about the next 24 hours of sobriety, or if that didn't work, the next hour of sobriety, and if that didn't work, the next 15 minutes of sobriety. In short, being taught to live in the moment, something that I had never done.

And those minutes, those hours and those days turned into weeks and I began to believe that I could stay sober. And that belief stemmed from actions that I was taking. Small steps at first like going to meetings which were followed by the action items of taking the steps themselves under the guidance of a sponsor. Understanding this simple formula for change was a huge step forward on the spiritual path. From that understanding stemmed obtaining an MBA, learning to the play the piano, starting a rigorous Yoga practice, joining a Yoga teacher training program and ultimately building a Yoga studio. In the larger picture though, I became willing to believe in me, and took the actions necessary that eventually led to the most important gift a human can give themselves, and that is faith in self, stemming from internal love, patience, compassion and understanding. We must remove the fears that are obstacles to growth for any forward movement to occur. We must have some sense of serenity as space to grow. We must have willingness to grow, belief that we can and then take the actions to do so.

I am hoping to record some guitar music in the next couple of years!

*Seattle, WA.* The computer screen read $559. It was February and I was trying desperately to get a flight in June to visit with family in Virginia and then travel to Vermont for a Yoga Festival. The flight was too much. My head starting spinning about the greed of the airline companies and how deplorable their customer service had become. This thought process was usually followed with bewilderment at how the government could allow a regulated industry to have four companies control 90% of the market and call it a free, competitive market. I then realized that record airline profits equal massive tax revenues and if the corporations and the government are happy, the consumer is always on the losing end. It's always about the money. Always.

My inner self kept telling me that I needed to be at that Yoga Festival. I had attended the one in Hawaii earlier in the year and it was a blast, but why Vermont? There were three more on the west coast a month after. It was nagging at me and had been nagging at me like a rock in my shoe for the couple months. I was starting to make justifications to pay extra for the ticket such as needing to see my family (whom I had already seen several this calendar year). I checked with one of the smaller airlines and paid the $400 for the ticket, and then proceeded to purchase another $300 in light camping gear, and another $700 on the Festival ticket. One thousand, four hundred dollars later I was going, and hadn't a clue why.

*Boston, MA.* A broken hearted female set the phone down on the verge of tears. She was in her late twenties and subject to heavy emotions and her friend had just bailed on her the day before a Yoga Festival in nearby Vermont. They were both going to explore themselves and get away from the city life for a few days. It was a short drive into the beautiful Vermont foothills and both of them had volunteered to work at the event in exchange for a pass they could use during their off hours. She was packed including a huge six man tent she had affectionately named "Bertha" along with blow up palm trees and two huge pairs of sunglasses. There was no way she could go alone; it was not her nature. Even though she recently had been slowly and begrudgingly moving down a spiritual path, driving to a Yoga Festival and camping there alone for four nights was out of the question. The next day she found herself driving down the Mass Turnpike blasting Margaretville on the radio headed to Vermont, feeling like someone else was driving and she was on the cruise control of life.

*Stratton, VT, The Yoga Festival.* The little tent city began to spring up at the bottom of the hill that in the winter time served as the base of the ski trails on this side of the mountain. The mechanical lift sat idle in the late afternoon sun on a small butte that rose from the parking lot at the entryway. The grass was fresh and green in early June and the fresh scent of pine from the trees winding up the hill was wafting through the yoga festival attendees as they staked out their claim to pitch their tent.

This would be home for the next four days. People, who had not met before set up their chairs, assisted each other with their tents and unloading their cars and chatted about the upcoming festival. "Is this your first Stratton?" a tall thin woman in painted on yoga tights asked a stocky man in his early twenties who looked more like he belonged at a college keg party than a yoga festival. "First time!! My girlfriend loves these events; she went to Aspen last year," he replied, barely acknowledging her question in the excitement of getting the camping gear organized. The people that were new were more obvious than the people who had been before, the yoga festival veterans had an air of been there, done that about them, but not in a condescending way. Their first impression just felt a little nonplus.

179

When I pulled up to the camping area I looked at the hill as a strategic place to be in case of rain, but instead was looking off to the right along the edge of the woods, which seemed more private. I was very much into quiet reflection on this particular trip and intended to keep to myself most of the time, enjoying my practice and going within. The universe had other plans for me but I was unaware of them at this point. I was just setting up shop near the woods when a very strong pull within me stopped me dead in my tracks and pointed me to the plateau. I had learned well enough at this point to listen to the voice within, so I moved camp to the far right end of the plateau, not thinking anything of it.

I set up my one-man tent, which was just large enough to hold me, and dropped the rental car back down in the parking lot. I had driven to Vermont from Buffalo where I was visiting family. The week prior I had spent in central Virginia at a lake house with family and friends so I was pretty well relaxed and had a lot of gratitude in my heart for the freedoms that were offered me, especially travel and experiences like this.

Upon returning to the camping area there were a group of people chatting in the center of the tents so I walked up and introduced myself. Steve was a yoga festival veteran who had been to many of these including the one a couple weeks prior. He was a local from just north of here. Steve was in his early 50's and looked incredibly healthy. This is normal for people that practice yoga. People that are serious about it and practice regularly and correctly very often look much younger than their age and have little body fat. People that practice yoga regularly also tend to live overall healthier lives including diet and limited environmental pollution from TV and advertising. Steve fit this description exactly. He had bright and gentle eyes and a friendly demeanor that soaked his presence. He was about average height with salt and pepper hair, broad shoulders and thick legs.

Rebecca was also a local and she had been to Stratton last year. While she was a little heavy for what one might think of for a yogi, it was all muscle. It is a common and misguided conception that people that practice yoga have to be thin and flexible, unfortunately driven by the society within which we live. She had a welcoming smile with long dark hair in a ponytail. Kim was wearing what I would later call 'Happy Kim face' as she was trying to explain to Steve that the hammer that she had could put the stakes in for his canopy. The hammer was pink and tiny and was only a hammer in a sense that it was shaped like one. Looking at it, I wasn't sure if it could hammer in a thumb tack. She was giggling and laughing, her hair was up in pigtails that looked like antennas sticking up off the top of her head. I loved her energy immediately, but didn't take notice of anything else at that point. I was still in my own little world and tired from the drive. After introducing myself and some small talk, the four of us decided to go to the ski village and grab some dinner.

The camping area was about a mile from the main resort and there was a bus that ran every 15 minutes or ample parking if one chose to drive. I offered to drive since I didn't drink. One of the many things I enjoyed about being sober was offering to be the designated driver. It was a nice act of service and a god way to pay back all the karma from my driving under the influence episodes.

Upon pulling into the parking lot, it was impressed upon me how different a ski resort looks and feels in the middle of the summer. It was a lot less populated for one. But it was odd to see people walking around in shorts and t-shirts in a place that during the winter time was far below zero and covered in a blanket of snow. The empty and unmoving ski lifts were a reminder that the population here was foreign during this time of year and everyone seemed just out of place. The resort area was a single pedestrian street lined with Victorian style shops. Above the shops were rooms for guests and the buildings on either side rose up for six floors. It was very quaint and offered the visitor the sense that they were in Switzerland or some other European ski destination. The altitude of the mountain was only 6,000 feet so not large by ski standards but the elevation drop from the top to the bottom was 4,000 feet so it had a nice drop.

We meandered down the street taking in the town for the first time and making the standard small talk, learning where we were from, what we did for a living and the usual discussions of how we identify ourselves as human beings. It was later than we thought and the restaurants were mostly closed so we found a bar that was still serving appetizers. We ordered a round of drinks and continued the process of getting to know each other.

"I would love to teach you some Acro Yoga" Steve offered this to the group as we were discussing the various types of yoga classes offered at the festival. Acro Yoga is partner based yoga where one partner on the ground (the base) balances the other partner in the air (the flyer). The flyer does most of the postures.

"When can we do that? It sounds amazing and fun." Kim was open to all the experiences here and had a beautiful enthusiasm about her. I was sitting on her left sharing a common side of a big table and estimated her age to be about 26. Steve and Rebecca were sitting to our right on another side of the table so that we formed an L.

"How long have you had your studio?" Kim asked me and I noticed how stunning and captivating her smile was. It made my heart smile just looking at her. I gave her the brief run-down of the studio and how it came to be without too much of the detail. Steve and Rebecca were now in their own conversation as I don't think they could hear me across the large table where we sat. We finished our drinks and seeing that it was late we headed back to camp.

The energy of the place and the people was very stimulating. It was much like the festival that I went to in Hawaii some months earlier. People that practice yoga tend to be positive and aware of their surroundings, and give off a general sense of love and ease. At these festivals that feeling is personified because everyone's energy is amped up. The jobs and the stress from everyday life are left behind for a weekend of mindful living and the practice of yoga.

When we arrived back at camp Rebecca and Steve said good night and Kim and I stayed up and chatted for a few more minutes, looking at the stars. We had no chairs to sit in and it was chilly so the conversation was short, but there was an unmistakable connection.

"How old are you?" She had been dying to ask me that all night, I thought to myself. I also asked the divine if it would be OK to lie just this once! The divine said no.

"I am 46." Her eyes got big and she laughed.

"I thought you were 36." She said this with a sly smile of disbelief on her face like I wasn't being exactly truthful and exaggerating my age to be older.

"Thank you! That is very sweet of you." I often have people mistake me for being much younger. I have a young face and keep my body in good condition, inside and out. I also had my hair dyed platinum blonde for the summer and it took some years off over my normal salt and pepper hair color. We said goodnight, but to this day, I feel like something was left unsaid that night. The immediate spiritual connection was overwhelming.

Kim was a volunteer at the festival, which meant she had to work about five hours a day checking people in to classes or helping with other duties three of the four days. She was free to practice on Sunday and outside of the times that she was volunteering. I had booked four yoga classes a day for all four days of the festival. First thing on my list for Thursday morning was aerial yoga. This is yoga hanging in the air on silks, much like at the circus. I then had a number of classes that ranged from Vinyasa flow to Yin to Nidra, the yogic sleep. The festival was set up with four primary class times throughout the day and each class time had about 20 classes to choose from. Walking into my second class on the first day I noticed that Kim was working the check in. How nice!

"Hey! Good to see you again. Enjoying the volunteer work?" She gave a big smile as she checked me in, the connection that was there last night immediately shining bright.

"I am. It's pretty easy actually. We do a lot of standing around in between classes. Is everyone getting together for dinner tonight?"

"That sounds like fun. How about we connect back at camp after the 2:00pm classes?" I actually had a 4:00pm class on the schedule but hanging out with her seemed more important.

"See you then," she said as she turned to assist other people check into the class.

That evening, the four of us went to the resort area again and found a pizza place that had an outdoor fire pit. The fire was warm and welcoming as a chill had set into the early June air. There were the usual musical chairs as the smoke blew inconsistently in all directions and never seemed to settle in one place. Kim, Steve and I sat in chairs near each other with an open view to the passersby and Rebecca was sitting on some rocks with her back to the path chatting up some people from Canada. Kim had a flowing white summer dress on with a strapless top and her hair was up in a high ponytail. Her smile radiated from beyond her face as she soaked in every moment of the festival. We took some pictures together and ordered drinks and appetizers while we enjoyed the warmth of the fire and the diverse company it provided. There were the people from Canada, a couple from Maine and three women from northern Vermont and everyone had the same positive vibe. These festivals were like that.

The energy was amped from the connection that we all had, and that connection was the practice of Yoga and what it did for us singularly and collectively. Yoga is about unity and these festivals were a living and breathing example of unity. Yoga did something different for each person; it was a very individualized practice, but at the core of that practice was striving for unity of self, which is universal. In each person, there was a different level of realization of this unity which is a good a definition of any as to where they are on their spiritual path.

How deep is your realization of self, or put another way, awareness of self? The question itself is as esoteric as the answer in that it cannot be measured quantitatively, and the realizations one can have about self are countless until complete unity of self is realized. This unity is the elimination of all duality, or becoming one with the universe.

We spent the evening getting to know each other more. It turns out that Steve was very hardcore about his practice and usually did at least one per day and was very involved in Yoga as a way of life. Kim worked as a caregiver in the Boston area and lived with three other people in a group house setting. She was from Boston and her parents still lived in a nearby suburb. Her practice had become more regular over the past year and the studio where she practiced had recommended this festival. The energy that Kim and I had together was uncanny and we both laughed at the "coincidence" that she was working one of the classes that I attended.

Friday morning came early. I had signed up for an 8:00 am class and got up at 6:30 so that there would be time for a shower and breakfast. After a light breakfast of fruit, granola and an energy drink I walked over to my class. Of the 20 classes in session in this time slot, Kim was working the door again. We gave each other a very eerie look at this point as coincidence was starting to border on an oddity.

She looked tired so I made her an energy drink and gave it to her to perk her up. She told me later that she had to turn away to blush.

We all spent Friday night at the same outdoor fire. Kim and I were looking at each other but neither of us was saying the obvious, which was the odd number of coincidences that kept bringing us into the same space. We started to tell each other of the strong draw that we had to come here and she mentioned how she almost didn't come after her friend had bailed. She said that she has no idea where she got the courage to come alone as it wasn't even remotely her nature.

I laughed nervously at this and wondered if I should share my experience with looking for a flight almost every day for two months to come here. I spent about $1,000 in time trying to save $150 on the flight, but knew I needed to be here, for a yet undisclosed reason. I told her. We spent the balance of the weekend together. From there she flew out to Seattle a month later to attend another Yoga festival in California where we enjoyed a glorious two-day road trip down and back. A month after that she moved to Seattle to start Yoga Teacher training, start a Reiki business at Ripple Yoga, and manage the space while I was in India for the next six months.

I have a reached a point in my spiritual life where I no longer argue with my inner guru. My experience is that when I practice turning my will and my life over the care of the divine every day, and when the time is taken to sit quietly and listen, that direction is given. We figure out our higher purpose in life, our Dharma, and we get happy. I got happy.

I got happy through the most challenging process I think any human can complete, and that is the process of honest self-examination. This was not done voluntarily of course; I was given the choice of death or recovery from death with painful self-examination. I feel truly blessed to have chosen, or have been chosen, to do the latter and live the life I have now. I have been largely freed of the misery of perception, or misperception, as it is.

I am responsible for everything that happens in my life, recognize it deeply, and also recognize that it is this acceptance of responsibility for my own life that is providing me with this happiness. I look out and see a world of victims, suffering in their own minds blaming the world for their woes, and the key to their suffering is locked inside them. This has always been the human condition, there are people that are freed and people that suffer, and it ebbs and flows like the sea of time.

I think that we are now in a dire state of the world with greed, selfishness and ego run amok having the upper hand. But I also feel the tide is turning, especially in America. People are getting fed up, and there is a feeling of undercurrent searching for something. That something may not be readily describable, but it is now my Dharma to describe it, to teach it. And that is virtue.

Humans suffer in the prison of their own minds from lack of virtue, and modern Western society and the model of capitalism practiced is a destroyer of virtue. As much as there is an undercurrent of seeking, there is an equal undercurrent of hatred, driven by the ignorance of a society dumbed down by its very own system. America has become the lowest common denominator in education, television, news reporting (if that is what anyone calls it these days) and parenting, to name a few. It is everyone's problem to fix, one person at a time, by looking in the mirror. It is not the government's problem, a corporate problem, the neighbor's problem. Each person in this world needs to understand that everything that happens to them, past, present and future is their doing. The only question that remains is, what are we going to do about it?

# Chapter 42

The cab pulled away from the ashram and I looked out the window at the street I had walked up and down barefoot a few hundred times. The same children were playing in the street; the same people were standing or sitting on their front porches. We passed the cow I had named Fred. He was always stammering back and forth from side to side of the road so I had given him a backstory that he had a drinking problem. This made me smile.

I hope Fred the cow gets the help he needs. To these people, I was just another student visiting the ashram, and probably left little impression upon them. There would be more students six months from now, everyone would be a year older, but life would be the same. New baby goats would be born, the same Bajans would be playing from the scratchy CD and circa 1970's speaker outside the local temple, beautiful chalk designs would adorn the entryways to the houses, and the rhythmic sound of the ocean lapping against the shore would blend into the daily life, hardly noticed by the inhabitants of this small fishing village.

But to me this place had made a deep impression. One that I hope never fades. I found new beauties inside me that I intend to nurture as the female dog in the ashram nurtures her fresh litter of puppies every six months. My body had changed; the hard western muscles from a lifetime of sports and sitting morphed into the soft and supple, but just as strong, muscles of a yogi. Where the fisherman sitting topless and smiling on his front porch just saw me as another student, I now saw him as a beautiful soul trying to find its way.

Maybe not this lifetime, but if he was fulfilling his Dharma, he would move upward and evolve, just like the rest of us. Evolution waited for no one. This place of beauty, this place where talking to God is not a long distance call, but a local one, has changed my perception of the world. India has its own special feel in the air, in the water, in the soil. The energy here is old and austere; there is a grace to it that can only be experienced. It is breathing in 10,000 years of history and the wisdom of a people that had everything figured out long before Christ was crucified for figuring everything out. It is connecting with the DNA of the universe if you are fortunate enough to pay attention.

I could feel the eyes of an older woman on me as we drove by. She waved and smiled, and I waved and smiled back. Three months earlier, I was petting one of her baby goats and she offered it to me, asked me if I wanted to drive it around on my bicycle. A simple act of beauty and sharing as she could see that it made me happy. As the car pulled out onto the main highway heading towards the airport, I lowered my head to my hands and cried. I cried for beauty, for love, for life, for this place, for the divine, for God's grace that I was given another chance at this life, and for this little slice of the world that gave so much to me. But mostly I cried because I was going home, to see the people I loved the most, and to share all the new love that I had found.

# Appendix One – The Twelve Steps of Alcoholics Anonymous

1. We admitted we were powerless over alcohol - that our lives had become unmanageable.

2. Came to believe that a Power greater than ourselves could restore us to sanity.

3. Made a decision to turn our will and our lives over to the care of God as we understood Him.

4. Made a searching and fearless moral inventory of ourselves.

5. Admitted to God, to ourselves and to another human being the exact nature of our wrongs.

6. Were entirely ready to have God remove all these defects of character.

7. Humbly asked Him to remove our shortcomings.

8. Made a list of all persons we had harmed, and became willing to make amends to them all.

9. Made direct amends to such people wherever possible, except when to do so would injure them or others.

10. Continued to take personal inventory and when we were wrong promptly admitted it.

11. Sought through prayer and meditation to improve our conscious contact with God as we understood Him, praying only for knowledge of His will for us and the power to carry that out.

12. Having had a spiritual awakening as the result of these steps, we tried to carry this message to alcoholics and to practice these principles in all our affairs.

## Appendix Two – The Eight Limbs of Ashtanga Yoga

**Yama** – Restraint of animal instincts; Morals

**Niyama** – Expansion of humanness; Ethics

**Asana** – State of being, often referred to as the physical practice

**Pranayama** – Control or restraint of energy and breath

**Pratyahara** – Control, restraint and fulfillment of senses

**Dharana** - Concentration

**Dyana** - Meditation

**Samadhi** – Cosmic consciousness

# Glossary of Terms

**Ahimsa** – Non-violence.

**Satya** – Truth or reality.

**Asteya** – Non-stealing.

**Brahmacharya** – Control of creative energy. Note that this Yama is not mentioned in this story but is included as a reference so that the list of Yamas is complete.

**Aparigrahah** – Non-greed.

**Sauca** – Purity and cleanliness.

**Samtosha** – Contentment.

**Tapas** – Discipline.

**Swadiyaya** – Self-analysis.

**Isvara Pranidana** – Turning over to our higher self.

**Satsangha** – group learning session and discussion with the Guru.

# About the Author

Sarvesh (formerly Gary) lives a Yogic life in Seattle, WA and loves to experience life through travel and different cultures as a paradigm for learning. We gain wisdom through experience with other human beings in other cultures, and begin to see through the characteristics of the different cultures to the unity that exists among us. We see that we are all the same essence of divinity. Sarvesh is the owner of Ripple Yoga, in the South Lake Union neighborhood of Seattle, WA and teaches classes there regularly. Prior to becoming a Yogi, Sarvesh was a corporate financial executive for 20 years in various technology companies. He earned a Bachelor's of Science in Business Management, Finance from the University of Maryland and a Masters of Business Administration, Executive Management from Washington State University. He has accumulated over 2,500 hours of intensive Yoga teacher training including completing the 6-month program at Ananda Ashram, ICYER in Pondicherry, India. Sarvesh is a passionate hockey player, volleyball player, vocalist, guitarist and pianist.

Do you have an inspiring story?  Check out our web site and email your story to Sarvesh.  We will post it and a photo to our blog for the community to read.  Through sharing our growth and inspiration, we create a beautiful ripple effect in the world.  If you enjoyed this story, please let people know about it and carry the message of hope and inspiration that it offers.  Share it on Facebook, Instagram or write a review!

## Websites and Social Media

www.200000oms.com

www.sarveshnaagari.com

www.rippleyoga.com

## Facebook

www.facebook.com/rippleyoga

www.facebook.com/200000oms

www.facebook.com/sarveshnaagari

## Instagram

@rippleyoga

66911326R10113

Made in the USA
Charleston, SC
31 January 2017